如果灵魂不能言语，
如果灵魂没有语言，
如果灵魂是机体死亡后的漂浮，
那么，
彼岸性文本就是灵魂奥义的传授：
它把晦暗幽闭的窒息变作虔诚无言的静思；
它把必然死亡变成不朽生灵；
它把丧葬仪式变为天堂圣典；
它把一切灵魂的飘荡变成一座远景式的迷宫；
它把冥冥世界变为永远安宁的终极王国。

——胡志颖

If the soul cannot speak,
    if it has no language,
    and if it is something floating after the death of an organism,
    then a text with Paramitality will be something imparting abstruse ideas of the soul.
It transforms gloomy and incarcerate suffocation into pious and speechless meditation,
    inevitable death into eternal life,
    funeral rites into holy ceremonies in the paradise,
    the floating of all souls into a labyrinth in a distant view,
    and the unseen world into an ever-peaceful ultimate kingdom.

— Hu Zhiying

海风出版社

HAIFENG PUBLISHING HOUSE

胡志颖作品集

A Collection of Works by
Hu Zhiying

海风出版社
HAIFENG PUBLISHING HOUSE

目　录

016　孤独行者的自由（序一）⋯⋯⋯⋯⋯⋯⋯⋯⋯⋯⋯⋯⋯⋯⋯⋯⋯⋯⋯⋯⋯⋯⋯⋯⋯⋯⋯⋯⋯⋯⋯⋯⋯⋯⋯⋯⋯⋯⋯　高名潞

018　灵魂深处的景观（序二）⋯⋯⋯⋯⋯⋯⋯⋯⋯⋯⋯⋯⋯⋯⋯⋯⋯⋯⋯⋯⋯⋯⋯⋯⋯⋯⋯⋯　意大利驻广州总领事馆文化处

020　一位非传统的个人主义艺术家：论胡志颖（序三）⋯⋯⋯⋯⋯⋯⋯⋯⋯⋯⋯⋯⋯⋯⋯⋯⋯⋯⋯⋯⋯⋯⋯　迪迪埃·赫希

022　20世纪80年代
　　　研究
　　　048　找回历史的高度 ⋯⋯⋯⋯⋯⋯⋯⋯⋯⋯⋯⋯⋯⋯⋯⋯⋯⋯⋯⋯⋯⋯⋯⋯⋯⋯⋯⋯⋯⋯⋯⋯⋯⋯⋯⋯⋯　张文海
　　　050　水墨语言的先天综合性 ⋯⋯⋯⋯⋯⋯⋯⋯⋯⋯⋯⋯⋯⋯⋯⋯⋯⋯⋯⋯⋯⋯⋯⋯⋯⋯⋯⋯⋯⋯⋯⋯⋯　胡志颖

054　20世纪90年代
　　　研究
　　　134　文化权力的无常——解读胡志颖 ⋯⋯⋯⋯⋯⋯⋯⋯⋯⋯⋯⋯⋯⋯⋯⋯⋯⋯⋯⋯⋯⋯⋯⋯⋯⋯⋯⋯⋯　王璜生
　　　138　志颖和他的画 ⋯⋯⋯⋯⋯⋯⋯⋯⋯⋯⋯⋯⋯⋯⋯⋯⋯⋯⋯⋯⋯⋯⋯⋯⋯⋯⋯⋯⋯⋯⋯⋯⋯⋯⋯⋯⋯　吕品田
　　　142　一个人的海市蜃楼——关于胡志颖和他的艺术 ⋯⋯⋯⋯⋯⋯⋯⋯⋯⋯⋯⋯⋯⋯⋯⋯⋯⋯⋯⋯⋯⋯　杨　卫

144　21世纪
　　　研究
　　　198　中国画家胡志颖以培根赢得声望 ⋯⋯⋯⋯⋯⋯⋯⋯⋯⋯⋯⋯⋯⋯⋯⋯⋯⋯⋯⋯⋯⋯⋯⋯⋯⋯⋯　埃德·麦科马克
　　　200　胡志颖艺术中形式的含义、个人宗教与培根问题 ⋯⋯⋯⋯⋯⋯⋯⋯⋯⋯⋯⋯⋯⋯⋯　罗宾·佩卡姆、胡志颖
　　　204　胡志颖的崇高美学 ⋯⋯⋯⋯⋯⋯⋯⋯⋯⋯⋯⋯⋯⋯⋯⋯⋯⋯⋯⋯⋯⋯⋯⋯⋯⋯⋯⋯⋯⋯⋯⋯⋯⋯　鲍　栋

208　装置作品
　　　研究
　　　222　关于《世纪遗恨录》系列装置 ⋯⋯⋯⋯⋯⋯⋯⋯⋯⋯⋯⋯⋯⋯⋯⋯⋯⋯⋯⋯⋯⋯⋯⋯⋯⋯⋯⋯⋯⋯　胡志颖

224　年表
　　　238　附录：批评家、策展人、收藏家、经纪人简介

CONTENTS

017　**Freedom of a Lonely Passenger (Preface I)** ⋯⋯⋯⋯⋯⋯⋯⋯⋯⋯⋯⋯⋯⋯⋯⋯⋯⋯⋯⋯⋯⋯⋯⋯ Gao Minglu

019　**Landscapes of the Soul (Preface II)** ⋯⋯⋯⋯⋯⋯⋯⋯⋯⋯⋯ The Cultural Office of the Consulate General of Italy in Guangzhou

021　**An Artist as Unconventional Personality: On Hu Zhiying (Preface III)** ⋯⋯⋯⋯⋯⋯⋯⋯⋯⋯⋯⋯⋯⋯ Didier Hirsch

022　**Works from the 1980s**
　　Studies
　　049　Resuming the Proper Height of History ⋯⋯⋯⋯⋯⋯⋯⋯⋯⋯⋯⋯⋯⋯⋯⋯⋯⋯⋯⋯⋯⋯⋯⋯ Zhang Wenhai
　　052　The Congenital Comprehensiveness of Ink and Wash Language ⋯⋯⋯⋯⋯⋯⋯⋯⋯⋯⋯⋯⋯⋯ Hu Zhiying

054　**Works from the 1990s**
　　Studies
　　136　The Transiency of Cultural Power — Reading Hu Zhiying ⋯⋯⋯⋯⋯⋯⋯⋯⋯⋯⋯⋯⋯⋯ Wang Huangsheng
　　140　Zhiying and His Paintings ⋯⋯⋯⋯⋯⋯⋯⋯⋯⋯⋯⋯⋯⋯⋯⋯⋯⋯⋯⋯⋯⋯⋯⋯⋯⋯⋯⋯⋯⋯ Lv Pintian
　　143　The Mirage of a Single Person — About Hu Zhiying and His Art ⋯⋯⋯⋯⋯⋯⋯⋯⋯⋯⋯⋯⋯ Yang Wei

144　**Works from the 21st Century**
　　Studies
　　199　Chinese Painter Hu Zhiying Makes His Bones with Bacon ⋯⋯⋯⋯⋯⋯⋯⋯⋯⋯⋯⋯⋯⋯ Ed McCormack
　　202　Meaning of Forms, Personal Religion and Issues about Francis Bacon in Hu Zhiying's Art:
　　　　An Interview ⋯⋯⋯⋯⋯⋯⋯⋯⋯⋯⋯⋯⋯⋯⋯⋯⋯⋯⋯⋯⋯⋯⋯⋯ Robin Peckham and Hu Zhiying
　　206　The Sublime Aesthetics of Hu Zhiying ⋯⋯⋯⋯⋯⋯⋯⋯⋯⋯⋯⋯⋯⋯⋯⋯⋯⋯⋯⋯⋯⋯⋯⋯ Bao Dong

208　**Installations**
　　Studies
　　223　About the Installation Art Series *Century Remorse* ⋯⋯⋯⋯⋯⋯⋯⋯⋯⋯⋯⋯⋯⋯⋯⋯⋯⋯⋯ Hu Zhiying

224　**Chronology**
　　238　Appendix: A Brief Introduction to Critics, Curators, Collectors and Dealers

孤独行者的自由（序一）

高名潞

终极关怀问题仍然是中国当代艺术的主要问题。八十年代的终极关怀被九十年代以来的犬儒主义和重商主义所抛弃，但是，不等于它没有意义，也不等于中国当代艺术中没有保持渴望终极关怀的有识之士和保持终极关怀的艺术。在过去三十年，出现了一些坚持在日常冥想、创作和书写中追索终级关怀的文人艺术家，他们的共同特点是，不加入时尚，始终默默地在如何书写和视觉化这个终极关怀方面双向探索。胡志颖就是其中的一位。

书写和视觉语言的结合并不一定说明艺术家的思想深刻，书写也不一定等于证明艺术家的文人素质，但是，艺术家，作为现代知识分子的一部分，应当是文化创造的智者和思想者，这已经被中国几千年的书画艺术创作所证明。书写和冥想的深度创作思维之所以在现代社会受到怀疑，一方面是因为工业复制（以及它的衍生品——现成品和波普）在艺术样式方面所带来的冲击，另一方面，精神/物质二元对立的现代性话语强烈冲击了非西方包括中国的现当代艺术创作。启蒙主义以来，康德、黑格尔的以精神理念主导世界的哲学被西方后现代主义所颠覆，并走到了反面。物质与精神、人与自然的和谐被几个世纪人类征服外部世界的"宏伟"工程所破坏。个体的书写和冥想不再被认为是艺术创作的源泉，相反，时尚和复制等公众舆论被视为艺术品价值的判断标准。

但是，文人性和深度性创作必将在21世纪浴火重生。它有待当代的知识分子艺术家去建树。因为终极关怀是人类的永恒课题，特别是当全球化把物质主义和都市主义带到了世界各个角落以后，精神的自我放逐已经成为文化领域的有识之士所遵奉的信仰。

胡志颖是艺术理论的博士，也是有才气的艺术家，更是一位特立独行的冥想者。他的博士论文的内容是关于终极关怀的探究，即我们通常所说的"形而上"问题的思考。在他的书中，胡志颖用了"彼岸"的概念去概括的理念。他在书中充分地讨论了东方的哲学和文艺理论中的形而上的问题。尽管我认为彼岸的概念太容易让我们想到基督教精神和西方古典哲学的终极关怀，同时也很难摆脱西方的现实和彼岸二元对立的旧思维模式，但是，胡志颖把它放到东方文化的系统中进行解读和比较，我认为是非常有意义的。特别是在当代中国缺少形而上热情的时候，提出对"彼岸"的新解更是当务之急。

无论是形而上、终极关怀还是彼岸，其实在东方传统中，它们的文化属性要远远大于宗教属性和社会属性。中国人讲文化，其中已经包含了宗教和政治的意味。"文"对于中国人而言，有太多的意思，它不仅仅指那些具有物质外观的文化形态。它更是一种精神和终极关怀。南宋邓椿说："画者文之极也！"文人画之所以能在中国诞生必定和中国人所理解的文化内涵有关。

胡志颖的艺术创作大体走过三个阶段。八十年代的水墨画是大山大水，和这个时代的学者水墨，也就是那种我称之为"宇宙流"水墨的风格是一脉相承的。其特点是追求宏伟气势。胡志颖九十年代的绘画是符号的集成。想超越山水对表现文化象征性的局限性，转而直接融入文化符号，多种符号的拼合造成多义性，甚至山水的峰回路转也被改造为某种寓意性符号。近年来，胡志颖把符号和培根的画风结合，其实，胡志颖主要地运用了培根的"体积"形式，而扬弃了培根的"身心"主题。他把主题置换为终极思考的文化主题。胡志颖的"个人宗教"倾向导致对培根的执著追寻的崇敬，同时，胡志颖本能所具有的文化信念决定了他选取的形象资源更加自由和多样。

当代艺术走到今天，最需要的是自由。可是这个自由既不是那种标榜政治身份的意识形态的陈词滥调，因为它已经被历史证明很多是假的。也不是犬儒主义的跟风飘移，因为它终究是醉生梦死。自由来源于个人的慧根、定力和良心（社会良心和人性良心），这决定了具有自由的人永远无法被标签化和面具化。正是这个个体的深度性和独立性才能真正地表现自由，因为自由永远不是从外部来的，它是内在的生成，它来自自由的品质本身。所以，从这个意义上讲，自由永远不属于流行大众，而只属于孤独的行者。

二〇一一年三月

Freedom of a Lonely Passenger (Preface I)

By Gao Minglu

Ultimate concern remains a main problem of Chinese contemporary art. Ultimate concern of the 1980s has been abandoned by Cynicism and mercantilism of the 1990s, but it does not mean that it is no longer meaningful or that there are no men of insight who keep longing for ultimate concern or art that maintains ultimate concern in the field of Chinese contemporary art. In the past 30 years there have appeared some scholar artists who have persisted in seeking ultimate concern in their everyday meditation, creation and writing and who have the common characteristic of keeping away from fashion and making two way exploration in writing about and visualizing ultimate concern. Hu Zhiying is one of them.

The combination of writing and visual language is not necessarily an indication of the profoundness of an artist's thinking, and writing is not necessarily a testimony of an artist's literati quality. However, as part of modern intellectuals, artists should be wise men and thinkers in the creation of culture, as is proved by painting and calligraphy creation in the past thousands of years in China. The reason why the profound creative thinking embodied in writing and meditation is questioned in modern society is that industrial duplication (and its derivatives — ready-made and pop art) has affected art forms on the one hand and that the modern discourse characterized by binary opposition between spirit and material has a strong impact on non-western (including Chinese) modern and contemporary artistic creation on the other. After the advent of didacticism, the philosophy of Kant and Hegel according to which the world is dominated by the idea of spirit was subverted by Western postmodernism and went to its opposite. The harmony between material and spirit and between man and nature was destroyed by mankind's centuries-long "magnificent" project to conquer the external world. Writing and meditation by individuals are no longer considered to be the source of artistic creation; on the contrary, the public opinions such as fashion and duplication are regarded as the standard for judging the value of a work of art.

However, scholarly and profound creation will surely revive in the 21st Century and its revival is to be promoted by contemporary intellectual artists. Because ultimate concern is an eternal subject of mankind, especially after globalization brings materialism and urbanism to all corners of the world, spiritual self-exile has become the belief followed by men of insight in the field of culture.

Hu Zhiying is not only a doctor in art theory but also a talented artist and an independent meditator. His doctoral dissertation is an exploration of ultimate concern, that is, reflections on what we usually call "metaphysical" problems. In his book, Hu Zhiying sums up his ideas in the concept of "Paramita". There he gives a full discussion of the metaphysical problems in Oriental philosophy and theory of art and literature. Although we think that the concept of Paramita (the other shore) too readily suggests to us Christianity and ultimate concern in Western classical philosophy and that, at the same time, it is hard for this concept to break away from the old Western mode of thinking about the binary opposition between reality and the other shore, I think it is of great significance that Hu Zhiying attempts to expound it and to make some comparisons within the system of Oriental culture. Especially when there is a lack of enthusiasm for metaphysical thinking, it is an urgent matter to put forward a new explanation of "Paramita".

Whether it is metaphysics, ultimate concern or Paramita, as a matter of fact, in Oriental tradition, its cultural attribute far outweighs its religious and social attribute. Culture, as the Chinese understand it, already includes religious and political implication. For the Chinese, "culture" has too many meanings. It is a kind of spirit and ultimate concern, rather than merely those cultural forms with material appearance. Deng Chun of the Southern Song Dynasty said, "Painting is an extreme form of culture." The appearance of literati painting in China necessarily had something to do with the connotation of culture as the Chinese understand it.

Hu Zhiying's artistic creation, on the whole, has experienced three stages. His ink and wash paintings of the 1980s depict grand mountains and rivers. They and the scholarly ink and wash paintings of that era, that is, the style of what I call ink and wash paintings of "flow of universe", can be traced to the same origin. They are characterized by the pursuit of tremendous momentum. His paintings of the 1990s are integration of symbols. He tried to surpass the limitation of landscape painting in expressing cultural symbolism and to incorporate cultural symbols directly instead. The piecing together of various symbols leads to ambiguity and even the twists and turns of mountain paths in his landscape paintings are transformed into some symbols with implications. In recent years, Hu Zhiying has combined symbols with Francis Bacon's style of painting, but in fact, he has mainly made use of Bacon's form of "volume" and abandoned his theme of "body and mind". He has substituted the cultural theme of ultimate thinking for Bacon's original theme. Hu Zhiying's personal religious tendency leads to his reverence for Bacon's persevering pursuit, and at the same time Hu's inherent cultural conviction has determined the freedom and diversity of his choice of resources of image.

What contemporary art needs most today is freedom. This freedom, however, is neither the ideological cliché used to advertise one's political identity, for it has been proved to be false in many cases by history, nor the Cynical attitude of following the herd, for it means, after all, leading a befuddled life. Freedom comes from a person's root of wisdom, perseverance and conscience (social conscience and human conscience). This determines that a man with freedom will never be labelized or stereotyped. It is an individual's profoundness and independence of this kind that make it possible to truly express freedom, for freedom never comes from external things but instead it comes from within, and from free quality itself. In this sense, therefore, freedom never belongs to common people who follow the trend but only belongs to lonely passengers.

March, 2011

灵魂深处的景观（序二）

意大利驻广州总领事馆文化处

在过去15年中，胡志颖一直在探索"文化反差"。直到20世纪90年代末，他将对传统中国绘画的深入阐释与对当代焦虑的表现相融合，创作了富有特色的"灵魂深处的景观"。近来他又专注于现成品与西方表现主义画派，这是那种最初追求的进一步发展。

胡志颖将中国传统山水画的象征体系与逐渐呈现出来的国际当代艺术风格的折衷主义相结合。在艺术家看来，被再现的形象与现实世界是同等的，而不仅仅是对它的记录。因此，"文化反差"既是一种抽象的知识，又是一种具体可感的知识。

胡志颖的巨幅绘画综合了很多种物体图像：他的富有想象力的透视常常使前景的物体与背景的物体相切换。传统绘画的和谐构图遭遇了当代灵魂的幽暗港湾。当观众试图领略众多意象的古代原型时，他们很可能被那梦幻般的绘画境界所迷住而不能自拔。

画布或者木板上的架上绘画使用了诸如墨、油彩与丙烯以及金粉与银粉、中国大漆等传统材料。这些不同的材料使得不同的形象更加充实，人们很容易将光滑的表面与我们过着平凡生活的世界的光明然而又不稳定的现实相联系。

同时，那些辉煌的前景中的现实暗示着隐藏在令人眼花缭乱的表面下的幽暗、神秘的世界。无论我们观赏《内典录》、《文字》还是其他系列，绘画语言都将抽象和具象融合在一种深邃的意境之中。

富有想象力的探究的不同系列其数目渐增，它们是《文字》、《数学》、《天文》、《方程式》、《原子》、《内典录》和最近的《重造培根》。激越的笔法和强烈的色彩之间的剧烈对比，同样表现了我们遭到忽视的灵魂王国的那些非传统的易变而非凡的图像。

二〇〇九年十一月十一日

Landscapes of the Soul (Preface II)

By The Cultural Office of the Consulate General of Italy in Guangzhou

In the last 15 years Hu Zhiying has been exploring a "culture contrast". Until the end of the 1990s he blends a penetrating interpretation of traditional Chinese painting with the representation of the contemporary anxiety, producing a characteristic "landscapes of the soul". The recent concentration on ready-made and Western expressionist school is a further development of that original concern.

Hu Zhiying combines the symbolism of the Chinese traditional landscape painting and the unfolding eclecticism of the international contemporary art styles. In the view of the artist, the represented images are as equivalent to the real world and not merely a document of it. The "culture contrast" is thus both an abstract and a perceptible knowledge.

The large painting of Hu Zhiying synthesis the images of many kinds of objects: his imaginative perspectives frequently switch the objects in the background with those in the foreground. The harmonic compositions of the traditional paintings crash into the dark creeks of contemporary souls. When the viewers try to discern the archaic prototypes in a multitude of imagines, they are likely to lose themselves in the dreamlike painted realm.

The easel paintings on canvas or board use conventional materials like ink, oil and acrylic colors, as well as gold and silver power, and Chinese Varnish. These various materials add substance to the diverse images and the glossy surface are easily identifiable with the bright yet unstable reality of the world in which we live our common life.

At the same time, those brilliant foreground realities imply a dark, mysterious world lurking beneath a dazzling surface. Either we look at *Buddhist Scriptures*, *Characters* or other series, the pictorial language blends abstraction and figuration in a profound artistic conception.

Progressive numbers identify the different series of imaginative researches, named *Characters*, *Mathematics*, *Astronomy*, *Equations*, *Atoms*, *Buddhist Scriptures* and the recent *Remake Bacon*. The vehement contrast between an intense brushwork and the strong colors similarly display those non-conventional changeable and extraordinary images of our ignored soul kingdom.

November 11, 2009

一位非传统的个人主义艺术家：论胡志颖（序三）

迪迪埃·赫希

胡志颖是我赞赏的艺术家的典型。

从他1989年的早期纸上水墨作品到他最近的向培根表示敬意的作品，他一直不墨守陈规，而是不断尝试将西方与东方影响的精髓融合起来。他从未有过机械的做法，联想有时是微妙的或者是明显的，但总是充满想象力。

在他所使用的混合媒介中，有时可以看到不同文化的融合。时常，这种融合通过画的母题表现出来：抽象/具象，表现主义/道教，中国符号/西方符号，等等。《天风海雨》（1989年）是宇宙论的和神秘的宣纸水墨作品，将书写、符号与艺术结为一体。它是那种释放了观者潜意识中的强有力的意象的作品，与罗夏墨迹试验不无相似。《文字之一》和《文字之二》（1992年）是油彩与丙烯、银粉与金粉、水墨、中国大漆与清漆的巧妙结合，它吸引住观者，使其心醉神迷。《数学之二》（1994年）和《内典录之二》（1997年）是自然图像、人类图像和抽象图像的复杂的但完美地平衡的世界，将超现实主义的影响和中国的影响奇妙地交融在一起，表现了迷人而又恐怖的美。《重造培根——女子角斗》（2005年）是对培根表达的敬意，同时又是一种戏仿。它通过添加增强或减弱暴力的元素进一步扭曲了培根的标志性的扭曲形象。

在我看来，胡志颖是终极的真正的艺术家，具有强烈的个人特性和强悍的不妥协的个性。他具有强烈的深思熟虑的方向意识，不过他总会使观者感到惊奇不已。

他在发挥他的天赋只为了满足一种强烈的（并且是合理的）自尊感。人们不得不想到晚期才得到承认的那些著名的19和20世纪的前卫艺术家们所走的孤独的道路。

总之，胡志颖的风格和艺术生涯显然没有大部分新潮流中的当代艺术（包括中国与西方）的特征，而与那些最终留下巨大的历史遗产的大师要接近得多。

二〇〇八年六月二十八日

An Artist as Unconventional Personality:
On Hu Zhiying (Preface III)

By Didier Hirsch

Hu Zhiying is the prototype of the artist that I admire.

From his early inks on paper in 1989 to his recent homage to Bacon, he has always traveled off the beaten path, but in a continuous attempt to combine the essence of western and eastern influences. He never had a mechanistic approach, and the associations can be subtle or obvious, but always imaginative.

The blending of the cultures can sometimes be seen in the mixed media he is using. Most of the time, it shows through the themes of the painting, abstraction / figuration, expressionism / Daoism, Chinese / western characters, etc. *Nature's Mystery* (1989) is a cosmic and mystic ink on Chinese paper with a conjunction of writing, symbols, and art. It is the kind of work that unleashes powerful images in the subconscious of the viewer, not unlike a Rorschach ink-blot. *Characters I* and *II* (1992) are masterful combinations of oils and acrylic, silver and gold powder, ink, lacquer and varnish which cast a spell upon the viewer and hold him spellbound. *Mathematics II* (1994) and *Buddhist Scriptures II* (1997) are complex but perfectly balanced worlds of natural, human, and abstract images, wonderfully blending surrealistic and Chinese influences, and expressing enchanting but terrifying beauty. *Remake Bacon — Female Wrestling* (2005) is homage to Bacon and a parody at the same time. It further distorts the trademark distorted figures of Bacon by adding elements which either reinforce or attenuate the violence.

To me, Hu Zhiying is the ultimate authentic artist, with a fierce individualism and a powerful no-compromise personality. He has a strong well thought — out sense of direction, although he will always surprise the viewers.

He is using his talent to solely satisfy a strong (and justified) sense of self-worth. One has to think of the solitary path followed by famous nineteenth and twentieth avant-garde artists who were recognized on the late.

In all that, his style and career are clearly uncharacteristic of that of most of the new wave of contemporary art (both Chinese and Western) and much closer to those who have ended up leaving a huge historical legacy.

June 28, 2008

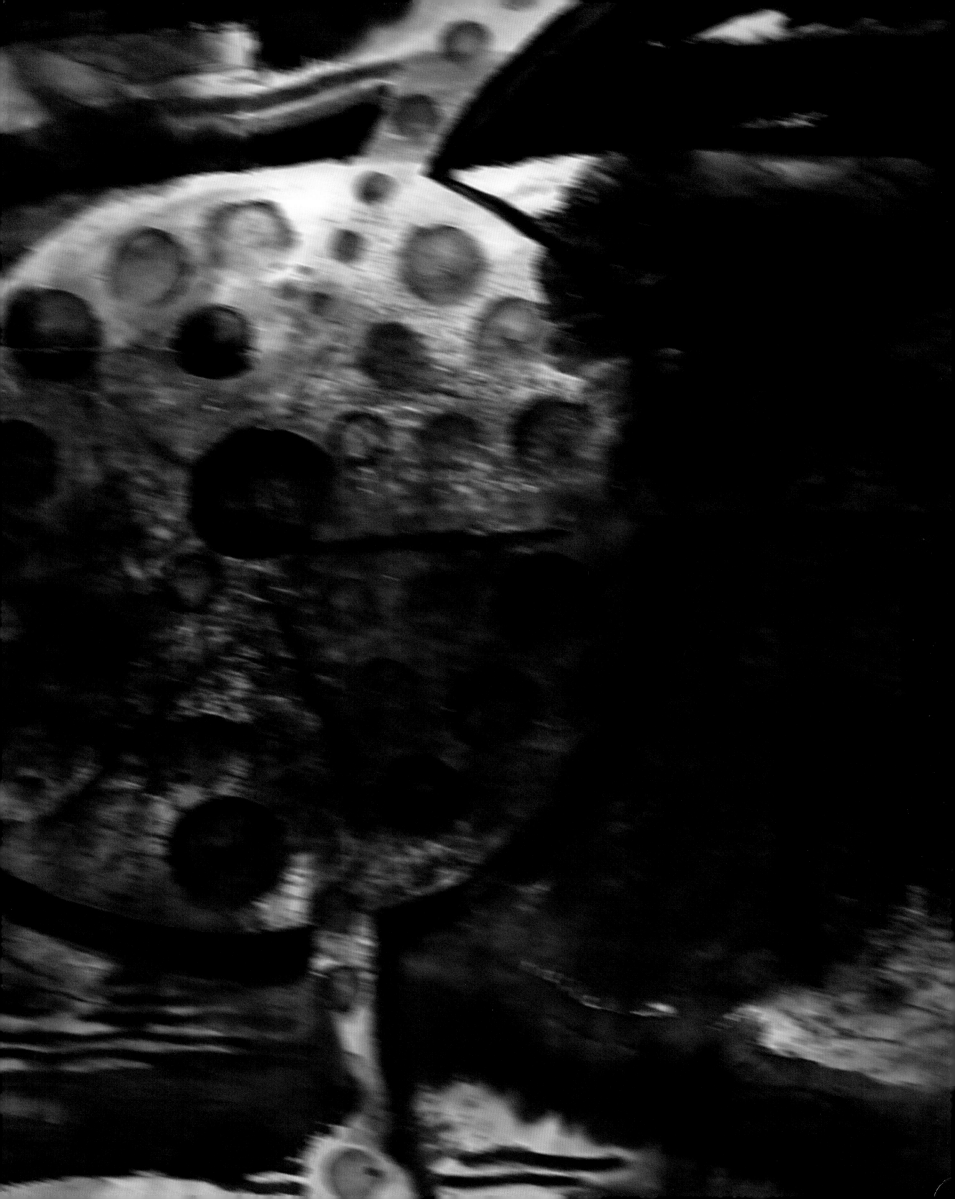

20世纪80年代
Works from the 1980s

胡志颖80年代的作品在美术史的互文关系中是很有意义的，是很有
代表性的，很强的。

——邹跃进

Hu Zhiying's works of the 1980s are significant in the intertextual relations of
art history. They are representative and powerful.

— Zou Yuejin

天风海雨，1989，宣纸上水墨，182×960cm
Nature's Mystery, 1989, ink and wash on rice paper, 182 × 960 cm

天风海雨（局部 一）
Nature's Mystery (detail 1)

心象的出场提供的是脱离任何现实感受的、不再现任何东西的虚幻；既近在咫尺又远在天涯；既空虚又完全；浮现和繁衍各种心象——没有自我控制和检审能力的心象。

想象属于一种未分化的内在体验。然而，主体必须借助于自然客体的轨道来描述这种形式的想象。而想象之文本形式企图把理性认知的自然阈限与想象分开，使二者毫不相关，毫无交流，似乎自然客体已不复存在。在此情形下，突破现实世界的限制，传达出一种神圣性的本质。

直觉的心象联系着幻觉，正是这种联系充实了虚幻的影像，把客观化的文本形式和捉摸不透的内容结合了起来，而这"充实"恰恰是极度虚无的变相。

——胡志颖

What is provided by the presence of mental images is something illusory that is divorced from all actual sensation and represents nothing. It is close at hand and also far away at the end of the world; void and also substantial. Various mental images emerge and multiply — mental images unable to control and examine themselves.

Imagination belongs to a kind of undifferentiated inner experience. However, the subject can only describe the imagination in this form with the aid of natural objects. Yet the textual form of imagination tries to separate the natural threshold of rational cognition from imagination, making them totally uninterrelated and without any mutual communication as if natural objects no longer exist. Under this condition, the limits of the real world are broken and a divine essence is conveyed.

Intuitive mental images have a link with illusion, and it is this link that substantiates illusory images and combines the objectivized textual form with the elusive content. This "substantiation" is nothing but a disguised form of extreme nihility.

— Hu Zhiying

天风海雨（局部二）
Nature's Mystery (detail 2)

大昭寺印象，1989，高丽纸上水墨，200×400cm
The Impression of Zuglakang Monastery, 1989, ink and wash on Korean paper, 200 × 400 cm

胡志颖作品所蕴含的背景知识对于有历史眼光的观察者来说充满魅力。
——罗宾·佩卡姆

The contextual interest in Hu Zhiying's works is fascinating for the historically-minded observer.

— Robin Peckham

山水之一，1989，宣纸上水墨，198×194cm
Mountains and Waters I, 1989, ink and wash on rice paper, 198 × 194 cm

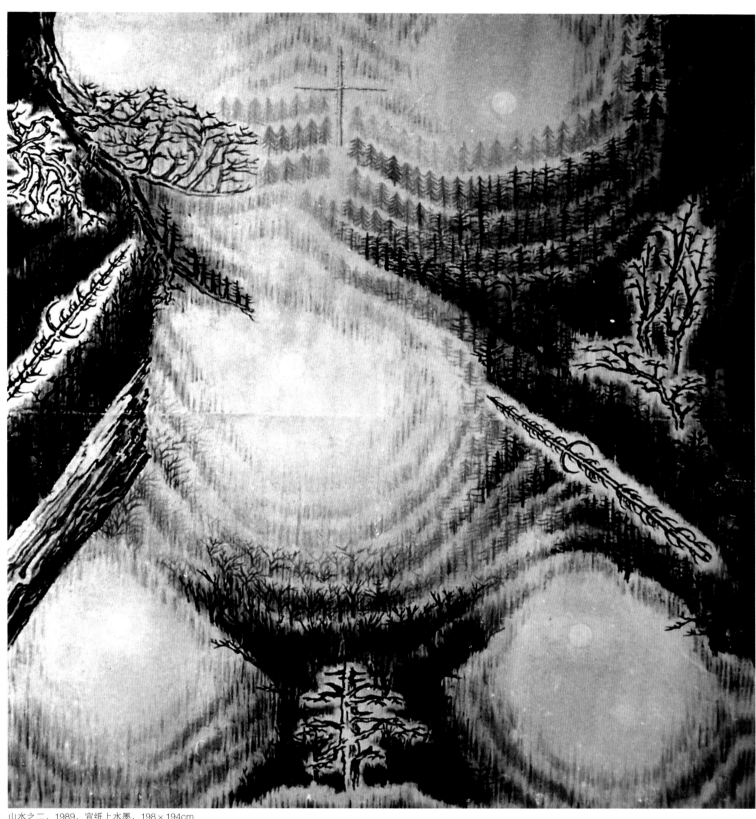

山水之二，1989，宣纸上水墨，198×194cm
Mountains and Waters II, 1989, ink and wash on rice paper, 198 × 194 cm

山水之三，1989，宣纸上水墨，198×194cm
Mountains and Waters III, 1989, ink and wash on rice paper, 198 × 194 cm

山水之四，1989，宣纸上水墨，198×194cm
Mountains and Waters IV, 1989, ink and wash on rice paper, 198 × 194 cm

透视，1989，宣纸上水墨，182×960cm
Perspective, 1989, ink and wash on rice paper, 182 × 960 cm

透视（局部）
Perspective (detail)

水墨语言的先天综合性从起因上讲不依赖于经验，逻辑上无须涉及经验。它显示人的非理性根源乃是原始的不可度量的综合性整体。创作过程则将先天综合演绎为个别或众多的个别。自稳的先天综合性经后天演绎变为不稳定的个别——互有区别的各个个别。后天的创作实际上在赋予先天综合语言以结构和意义，而这种言说的结构和意义不可避免地会产生歪曲——辞不达意或辞不完全达意。"整理成形"的水墨画的意义，其平面性片面地诠释了具有不可添加或减少的先天综合性水墨语言原本是自然立体的时空状态的特性。

——胡志颖

In terms of its origin, the congenital comprehensiveness of ink and wash language does not depend on experience, and logically need not to be related to experience. It shows that the source of the irrationality of mankind is a primitive and immeasurable comprehensive whole. The process of creation transforms congenital comprehensiveness into a particular or numerous particulars. Through the process of transformation the self-stable congenital comprehensiveness is changed into unstable particulars that are different from each other. The act of artistic creation is actually endowing the congenital comprehensive language with structure and meaning, and distortions will inevitably occur in such structure and meaning on account of the failure of words to convey properly or completely the meaning. The flatness of "shaped" ink and wash painting explains one-sidedly the character of the congenital comprehensive ink and wash language which nothing can be added to or subtracted from, that is, it is, in essence, in a natural and three dimensional temporal and spatial state.

— Hu Zhiying

天河，1989，高丽纸上水墨，200×400cm
The Galaxy, 1989, ink and wash on Korean paper, 200 × 400 cm

天河（局部一）
The Galaxy (detail 1)

天河（局部二）
The Galaxy (detail 2)

绘画 No. 1，1989，宣纸上硃砂、墨、油彩、丙烯，120×188cm
Painting No.1, 1989, cinnabar, ink, oil and acrylic on rice paper, 120 × 188 cm

绘画 No. 2，1989，宣纸上硃砂、墨、油彩、丙烯，120×188cm
Painting No.2, 1989, cinnabar, ink, oil and acrylic on rice paper, 120 × 188 cm

绘画 No. 3，1989，宣纸上硃砂、墨、油彩、丙烯，120×188cm
Painting No.3, 1989, cinnabar, ink, oil and acrylic on rice paper, 120 × 188 cm

绘画 No. 4，1989，宣纸上硃砂、墨、油彩、丙烯，120×188cm
Painting No.4, 1989, cinnabar, ink, oil and acrylic on rice paper, 120 × 188 cm

绘画 No. 5，1989，宣纸上硃砂、墨、油彩、丙烯，120×188cm
Painting No.5, 1989, cinnabar, ink, oil and acrylic on rice paper, 120 × 188 cm

找回历史的高度

——简评胡志颖作品《天风海雨》

张文海

对中国艺术界来说，'85新潮是艺术家们在艺术与政治的夹缝里的一次爆发。绵延千年的水墨画发展至此也有了决裂式的突变。此时，传统意义上的笔墨技巧与构图形式已无法诠释夹缝里挣脱出来的现代艺术理念。水墨艺术不再是梅兰竹菊式的咏物述怀，而是以水墨为载体，直接阐发艺术家个人的现代艺术观念。观念落实到画面，也必然导致技法与图式的突破。在观念、技法以及图式的突破性方面，胡志颖的《天风海雨》足以成为 '85新潮时期乃至当下的众多艺术家的可资借鉴者。画面之中水墨语言及图式的丰富性，不仅彰显了作者超前的现代艺术观念，更给人以充分的视觉刺激和精神征服。

传统水墨观念讲究"传物之神"。至唐代张彦远有"书画之艺，皆须意气而成"之说；始将艺术创作的主旨直指创作者之"意气"。但应该看到中国的水墨艺术直至通常意义上的近现代，画面中始终未能摆脱传神之"物"。至 '85新潮，中国水墨艺术借西方现代艺术的抽象观念，一跃而跳出了"物"的束缚，于画面中直呈创作者的"心象"。从此时起，借助西方现代艺术理念，为了在新的时代赋予"水墨"这传承千年的媒材以新的生命，从事现代水墨创作的个人和团体数不胜数。但纵览全局，能称之为上乘、无愧于时代的作品，却若晨星之寥，而胡志颖的《天风海雨》却是这晨星中极其难能可贵的一颗。《天风海雨》作于1989年，画幅长近十米，宽近二米。作者此时正值而立之年，雄姿英发，观念超前。这尤其反映在水墨绘画语言水乳交融、酣畅淋漓以及因之而来的画面的斑斓形象、磅礴气势之中。近十米的鸿篇巨制，既保持了整体的神秘辽阔，又不失局部灵活通透。充分地呈现了创作者澎湃而饱满的激情，使观者置于幽冥、异类的世界中而不能自拔。

胡志颖1989年在广州美院读研究生时和他的作品《天风海雨》
Hu Zhiying and his work *Nature's Mystery* in 1989 when he was a postgraduate student at Guangzhou Academy of Fine Arts

然而，回顾中国的现代水墨之路，让人扼腕叹息的是在摆脱了中国传统文化从观念到图式对水墨艺术的支撑之后，带来的却是大量的画面语言的孱弱无力；水墨艺术或沦为小情小调的抒情小品，或陷入不知所云的生涩局促之局面。就绘画而言，对艺术观念的阐述决不应意味着绘画语言表现力的减弱，因为绘画艺术首先应该是视觉艺术。好的视觉艺术必须具备视觉想象力。这样的作品通过自身画面的技法与图式，不仅彰显创作者的想象力，更应该给观众带来丰富的想象空间。要做到这一点，就要求艺术家在创作时对自己的画面语言进行不断地探索和丰富，而不应该满足于一蹴而就的画面效果。当下的中国绘画艺术，艺术语言苍白无力，对此，胡志颖一语道破："形式语言的贫乏，必然导致其所展示的观念的廉价。"

但水墨因其媒材性质而注定非常人所能驾驭。水至明，墨至暗，水墨无形而各居阴阳之极，调合二者必可造出万千之势象。然水墨无常，乃天地间至灵之物，运此二者若驾风驭雨，非天分过人者不能为之。胡志颖运此至灵之物于一人之管，一发而挥就《天风海雨》，以至柔之物为至刚之象，实时代之幸，乃 '85新潮时期诞生的经典现代艺术之作。

但遗憾的是现有的所有史料在涉及所谓现代水墨的章节里，从来没有胡志颖的《天风海雨》。这虽然与其本人不事张扬的性格有关，但对于艺术史的书写者来说，显然有失职之嫌。因为这段艺术史必然会因为胡志颖《天风海雨》的缺失而丧失应有的高度。对于《天风海雨》，有评论家认为创作者应该借现代水墨当时的兴起之势而多做几幅；其实未必，一张画足以撼动一个时代，得此足矣！

胡志颖是当代艺术家中卓然不群的一个，他和他的作品只属于艺术，但不属于任何一个艺术群体。

Resuming the Proper Height of History

— A Brief Comment on Hu Zhiying's *Nature's Mystery*

By Zhang Wenhai

To the art circles of China, the '85 New Wave means the artists have broken away from the narrow space between art and politics. A sudden radical change has also taken place in the art of ink and wash after its development of more than a thousand years. Now techniques of ink and wash and compositional forms in the traditional sense are incompetent to convey modern artistic ideas which have broken away from a narrow space. The art of ink and wash is no longer something in which one's feelings are expressed by means of depicting objects such as plum blossoms, orchids, bamboos and chrysanthemums, but instead, the artist's personal modern artistic ideas are elucidated directly with ink and wash as a carrier. Ideas, when embodied in the painting, will necessarily lead to a breakthrough in techniques and schemata. In terms of the breakthrough of ideas, techniques and schemata, Hu Zhiying's *Nature's Mystery* suffices to be something to be used as reference by the artists of the '85 period and even of present day. The richness of the language of ink and wash and schemata not only demonstrates the advanced modern artistic concepts of the artist but also provides visual stimulus and results in spiritual conquest.

The traditional concept of ink and wash stresses "conveying the spirit of the objects". Zhang Yanyuan of the Tang Dynasty had the saying that "ideas and spirit are indispensable in the art of both painting and calligraphy" and began to regard the "ideas and spirit" of the artist as the purport of artistic creation. But it should be seen that in the Chinese art of ink and wash, up to the modern times in the usual sense, the "objects" used to convey spirit were never cast off in the painting. In the period of '85 New Wave, with the aid of the abstract concepts of Western modern art, Chinese art of ink and wash shook off the yoke of "objects" at one go and the "mental images" of the artist were conveyed directly in the painting. Since then, innumerable individuals and groups have been engaged in the creation of modern ink and wash in an attempt to infuse new life into "ink and wash", the medium with a history of over a hundred years, with the aid of the modern artistic ideas of the West. However, making a general survey of the situation, we find that the works that can be described as being of superior quality and worthy of the times are as sparse as the morning stars, and Hu Zhiying's *Nature's Mystery* is a commendable one of these morning stars. *Nature's Mystery*, with a length of nearly 10 meters and a width of nearly 2 meters, was produced in 1989. Exactly at the age of thirty at that time, the artist was audacious, spirited, and forward-looking. This is reflected especially in the harmonious, lively and lucid language of ink and wash, gorgeous images, and the tremendous momentum of the painting. This monumental work, with a length of nearly 10 meters, is both mysterious and extensive as a whole and flexible and lively in detail. It fully manifests the surging passion of the artist, and the viewers are led to an inextricable, gloomy and fantastic world.

However, reviewing the course of development of Chinese modern ink and wash, we see with regret that after the connection between the art of ink and wash and Chinese traditional culture in concepts and schemata was shaken off, what has been brought about is the feebleness of the pictorial language. The art of ink and wash has been reduced to the level of lyric pieces conveying trivial sentiments or has degenerated into something unintelligible, crude and awkward. As far as painting is concerned, the exposition of artistic concepts should by no means imply the enfeebling of expressiveness of the pictorial language, for the art of painting should be, above all, a kind of visual art. Visual imagination should be contained in good visual art. This kind of works, through techniques and schemata, will not only demonstrate the imagination of the artist, but also provide the viewers with room for rich imagination. To achieve this goal, the artist is required to explore and enrich his pictorial language in the process of artistic creation and should not be satisfied with the superficial artistic effect achieved in one step. In present Chinese art of painting, the artistic language is feeble. Hu Zhiying lays bare the reason with one remark: "The meagerness of the form language of a work of art will necessarily result in little value of the idea it reveals."

However, the character of the mediums used in the art of ink and wash prevents ordinary people from mastering this art. Water is extremely clear and ink extremely dark. They are shapeless and are extremes of clear and dark things. When blended, they will necessarily produce countless effects. But water and ink are capricious and extremely flexible. To manipulate them is as difficult as to command the wind and rain and only people with extraordinary talent can do it. It is a good fortune of the times that Hu Zhiying, using these extremely flexible things, produced *Nature's Mystery*, a classical work of modern art of the '85 period. In this painting, he created most powerful images using softest materials.

But unfortunately, Hu Zhiying's *Nature's Mystery* is never mentioned in any chapter about so-called modern ink and wash in all historical data. Although this has something to do with the artist's unassuming personality, the writers of art history are evidently suspected of dereliction of duty. For the art history about this period will necessarily lose its proper height owing to the absence of accounts about Hu Zhiying's *Nature's Mystery*. Some critics thinks that Hu Zhiying should have taken advantage of the rising of modern ink and wash at that time and produced more works like *Nature's Mystery*. In fact that is not necessary, for a single painting suffices to shake an era. This one is enough!

Hu Zhiying is an outstanding contemporary artist. He and his works belong to art only, but not to any art group.

水墨语言的先天综合性

胡志颖

　　"水墨语言"是一个不得已而权且借用的名称，它在被表述（或被成形）之前是缄默的。本来在主体内被体验的性状使之无法用人工语言或中介性符号来表达其实质。水墨画的媒介——宣纸和水墨作为硬性的物质，是主体欲望（对水墨语言的体验）宣泄物化的试验载体。在此试验过程中，水墨语言变成了主体的新经验以及由此产生的知识——水墨画。以水墨再现的内省与宗教式冥思源于水墨语言，其不可名状融于先天悟性的个体机缘之中，与后天物质性相悖。自我意识（对先天水墨语言的感悟）对感觉施以综合，企图构成一个统一的水墨世界。主体在用水墨媒介创作形式时，意识到自身水墨语言的存在，这种反身存在须通过行为得以显现。然而，水墨语言本质上不与后天水墨画创作行为相沟通，亦非后天经验所能获得。其中的问题是隐而不显的：水墨语言自足的完善具有不可添加或减少的先天综合性。

　　由于人类先天综合语言的封闭的这种本性，才须借助后天的感官经验通过一定的媒介表现出来。用人工语言的词汇和符号——线条、浓淡、燥湿、形状等表达综合性先天水墨语言，使之变为新的经验，这是危险的——精神要素作用于感觉经验的材料是部分的而非必然的。也就是说，不必求助于经验的先天水墨语言是必然的、稳定的，而经验性水墨画创作及其结果是不稳定的，不是必然的。但这又是不得不投射出来以供艺术共同体成员审美认知的真理，否则，对他人来说，主体的先天水墨语言永远地处于彼岸的沉寂中不得而知。水墨画创作就是演绎先天综合性水墨语言，把彼岸拉回到此岸。物质性的水墨画是先天水墨语言与艺术共同体成员约定的人工语言相碰撞的产物。

　　水墨语言的先天综合性从起因上讲不依赖于经验，逻辑上无须涉及经验。它显示人的非理性根源乃是原始的不可度量的综合性整体。创作过程则将先天综合演绎为个别或众多的个别。自稳的先天综合性经后天演绎变为不稳定的个别——互有区别的各个个别。后天的创作实际上在赋予先天综合语言以结构和意义，而这种言说的结构和意义不可避免地会产生歪曲——辞不达意或辞不完全达意。"整理成形"的水墨画的意义，其平面性片面地诠释了具有不可添加或减少的先天综合性水墨语言原本是自然立体的时空状态的特性。

　　纯粹意识与从实践经验中得来的知识相对，以不同的方式而存在。水墨先天综合语言存在于藏有先天综合语言的主体之中，潜在地存在，以备适时地成功调用。后天经验所能获得的是技术，技术不是必然的，这正是创作主体并非在所有情形下都能成功地调用其先天水墨语言的原因。主体在实践经验中认识和掌握技术。水墨语言的先天综合性意味着拥有它的主体能够直接地沉思永恒、稳定的理式，引起对自己头脑中先前固有（存在）真理的回忆。这些真理的回忆都以主体获得特殊的或偶发的机会对这先天综合性语言的假设为前提，来诠释这先天语言存在的可能性。技术努力作为先天综合性水墨语言之桥梁，引发本来虚化的宗教式冥思，使水墨语言的实现成为可能。然而，"意态由来画不成"，水墨画最终不过是宗教式冥思的剩余而已。偶发性的宗教式冥思与行为性的技术制动互为表里，互为矛盾。无制动的偶发性流于语言的消失，而制动的外化将宗教式冥思中断，使水墨语言秩序化。偶发性有着先天的自然结构，技术制动使偶发性不至于漫无边际地任意流淌，二者相互渗透、交织、冲撞，主体企图尽可能使二者在结局中自然地相与为一。

　　先天综合性水墨语言具有原始性，非由他物所派生。先天综合性水墨语言是潜在的、非物质的、自稳的本原。它是知识必不可少的前提，提供关于可能经验的对象；水墨画则是可见的物化知识形式，它以本原为依托。一个存在（先天综合性水墨语言业已存在而非生成），与以此存在为依托在创作中产生的另一个存在（水墨画）不可能成为统一性的存在。水墨画作为其所言说的精神存在的另一种存在，并非先天综合性水墨语言的直接转化，仅仅是通过精神整体的消失，而产生的新的存在，在此过程中，两者之间存在着时间上的关系。假设的形式就是对本原的安排或组织。先天综合性水墨语言潜在地成为主体去创作的种种水墨画的动因。只有当潜在的本原通过感官经验在现实时空中给予一定意谓的形式时，它才能实际地成为被诠释的那个对象。换言之，只有当那个对象被整理成客观形式——水墨画时，才产生有效的真正知识，以供知识共同体成员进行审美认知。通过水墨画作品可能反证其所言说的对象是先天综合性水墨语言而非分析性艺术语言。而缺乏先天综合性水墨语言的创作主体则仅仅处于水墨技术的花样翻新、搞新名堂的钻牛角尖式的情形之中（这正是人们误以为水墨画可以通过后天努力趋向优质效果的原因所在）。此时，"完成"水墨画过程实质上是创作他画种——水墨画的替代形式。而其他艺术门类，如油画、装置、方案、视像、媒体等艺术，可在实践中获得经验，并不断地修正其艺术形式的结构，反过来再扩大自身的艺术审美的主观经验。这些艺术的创作主体所基于的是与物质世界有着千丝万缕联系的分析性艺术语言（这是一个与先天综合性语言相对的问题）。

　　后天水墨画创作无疑是对先天综合性水墨语言的本体存在（自在）的探求、研究，更确切地说是某种推测，它企图揭示他人未知、自己未明的关于主体内部的语言事实——一个无法求证于实践经验的事实。创作主体试图以内省经验或内省认知，并通过水墨媒介来凸现先天综合性水墨语言于光明世界。先天综合性水墨语言和水墨画是晦明化流动过程中的两个阶段。先天综合性水墨语言乃未成形质之前，而水墨画是成形质之后。水墨画的个别特定永远处于对先天综合性水墨语言的终极状态的表述过程中，是有限的物理世界的种种范型。无论如何，创作结果都是有限的和不可靠的。所有水墨画都是超感觉的精神整体的知识形式，是用有限的形式构成来解释不可度量的精神整体的企图。表现的个体内部感觉的先天综合性水墨语言与体现共相的物质（如水、墨、纸等媒介），二者的质料通然相异。所以，先天综合性水墨语言的意义不可能还原为任何一种可限定的意义形式，它也不是众多水墨画形式的总和。然而，缄默的水墨语言的先天综合性又只有当它显现为言语的具体形式时，其缄默的综合性才能在一定程度上被理解，它永远处于矛盾逻辑的框架之中。

因此，也必须看到，水墨画与先天综合性水墨语言并非如想象的那般彼此分离。水墨画把不可度量、难以言说的先天综合整体分解成某种单一的形式，其任务就是表明这些单一的形式如何依赖于整体的内在活动。水墨画作为内部整体世界的外在呈象，乃不完全的机械存在。水墨画能以多种形式述说水墨语言，是内部世界的种种不同展示和对照。主体反复创作水墨画是对内部精神整体世界的向往，从而导致用机械的形质解释精神境界的行为发生，把精神简单地归结为物质，试图给整体自然系统的精神以推动。更多次的创作，企图对整体自然系统予以更充分的解释。实际上，若干次水墨画创作的种种具体行为是对整体精神境界的再想象和不同看法，以变化的不稳定状态弥补以个别方式存在的水墨画的机械性之不足。

　　一切先天综合性水墨语言都是天赋主体的内在秉性。先天综合性水墨语言与可加于它的任何解释——水墨画及其批评理论——都没有什么必然关系。如前所述，先天综合性水墨语言原本是缄默的，是未经解释的系统（整体）。用人工语言和符号以若干不同的方式加以解释，即犯了赋予缄默以言语的错误，其错误在于用已被赋予意义的符号来推导意义。水墨画这一物质形式错误地假设为先天综合性水墨语言的摹本。其实，假设的形式（水墨画）是对精神语言的性质的简单无奈的理解。

　　水墨画一旦产生，将被审美认知再激活，使之可能产生大于自身的能量而作用于知识共同体成员——欣赏者、批评家、创作者本人和其他艺术家。所以，更为恰当的是：将水墨画看作水墨语言的逻辑效应，这种效应的力量来源于水墨语言的先天综合性。要使处于无法避免的矛盾难题中的错误缩小，可以通过增加各种类型的新符号，构造一些更精细的系统，从而在其中表达范围更广的意义，表达更多的可能世界，扩大水墨画的相对价值。

（原载《国画家》2000年第四期，中国美术家协会）

The Congenital Comprehensiveness of Ink and Wash Language

By Hu Zhiying

"Ink and wash language" is a name I cannot but borrow for the time being. It is tacit before being represented (or being given a shape). Its nature of being experienced inside the subject excludes the possibility of expressing its essence with artificial language or intermediary symbols. The mediums used in ink and wash painting, namely rice paper, ink and wash, as indispensable materials, are carriers of the experiment to give vent to and to materialize the desire of the subject (his experience of ink and wash language). In the process of this experiment, ink and wash language is transformed into new experience of the subject and the resulting knowledge, namely, the ink and wash painting. Reflections and religious meditations represented in ink and wash painting originate from ink and wash language, and its indescribable feature is blended with individual chance as opposed to the acquired materiality. Self-consciousness (perception of congenital ink and wash language) synthesizes the senses in an attempt to construct a unified ink and wash world. When the subject creates forms using the mediums of ink and wash, he comes to realize the existence of his own ink and wash language and this reflexive existence must be manifested through action. However, ink and wash language does not communicate with acquired ink and wash painting creation essentially, and cannot be acquired through experience either. Problems in it are not obvious: self-contained and perfect ink and wash language has its congenital comprehensiveness, and nothing can be added to or subtracted from it.

On account of this closedness, human congenital comprehensive language can only be manifested through certain mediums with the help of acquired sense experience. It is dangerous to express comprehensive congenital ink and wash language with vocabulary and symbols of artificial language — lines, degrees of density, dry and wet, shapes, etc. — and to transform it into new experience: spiritual elements can produce an effect only partially but not necessarily on materials of sense experience. In other words, congenital ink and wash language without the need of help from experience is necessary and stable, yet the creation of ink and wash painting based on experience and the result of this creation are unstable and not necessary. However, the congenital ink and wash language of the subject is something that has to be manifested for the aesthetic cognition of members of the art community, or it will be in obscurity on the other shore forever, unknown to others. To produce ink and wash paintings is to apply the congenital comprehensive ink and wash language and to draw it from the other shore back to this shore. The substantial ink and wash painting is the product of the collision between the congenital ink and wash language and the conventional artificial language of members of the art community.

In terms of its origin, the congenital comprehensiveness of ink and wash language does not depend on experience, and logically need not to be related to experience. It shows that the source of the irrationality of mankind is a primitive and immeasurable comprehensive whole. The process of creation transforms congenital comprehensiveness into a particular or numerous particulars. Through the process of transformation the self-stable congenital comprehensiveness is changed into unstable particulars that are different from each other. The act of artistic creation is actually endowing the congenital comprehensive language with structure and meaning, and distortions will inevitably occur in such structure and meaning on account of the failure of words to convey properly or completely the meaning. The flatness of "shaped" ink and wash painting explains one-sidedly the character of the congenital comprehensive ink and wash language which nothing can be added to or subtracted from, that is, it is, in essence, in a natural and three dimensional temporal and spatial state.

Pure consciousness and the knowledge acquired through practical experience are opposite to each other and exist in different ways. The congenital comprehensive language of ink and wash is latent in the subject to be brought into play successively at due time. What can be acquired through experience are techniques, which are not necessary, and this is just the reason why the creative subject cannot bring congenital ink and wash language into play successfully under all situations. The subject understands and masters techniques though practical experience. The congenital comprehensiveness of ink and wash language implies that the subject possessing it can meditate on eternal and stable ideas directly, arousing memories of truth previously inherent (existing) in his mind. These memories of truth explain the possibility of the existence of this congenital language on the premise that the subject gains a special or accidental chance to suppose this congenital comprehensive language. Technical efforts as a bridge leading to congenital comprehensive wash and ink language trigger off the obscured religious meditation, making it possible to materialize ink and wash language. However, "the subtle manner can never depicted thoroughly in a painting", ink and wash paintings are no more than remnants of religious meditation. Accidental religious meditation and behavioral technical control are interlinked and contradictory to each other. Uncontrolled accidentalness will lead to the disappearance of language while controlled externalization interrupts the religious meditation and puts ink and wash language in order. Accidentalness has its congenital natural structure and technical control prevents accidentalness from spreading without limit. They penetrate, interweave and collide with each other, and the subject tries to bring them into natural combination in the end.

Congenital comprehensive ink and wash language is original, not derived from other things. It is a latent, non-material and self-stable source. It is an indispensable premise of knowledge and provides objects for possible experience, while ink and wash painting is the visible and materialized form of knowledge and it depends on the source. One existence (congenital comprehensive ink and wash language has already existed, it is not generated) and another existence (ink and wash painting) that appears in the process of creation based on the first existence cannot be identical. Ink and wash painting as another existence as opposed to the spiritual existence it tries to convey, is not directly transformed from congenital comprehensive ink and wash language, but a brand new existence produced through the disappearing of the spiritual whole; in this process, there is a relation of time between them. The supposed form is the arrangement and organization of the source. Congenital comprehensive ink and wash language becomes latently the motivation of the subject to create various ink and wash paintings. Only when the latent source is given a form with certain significance through the experiences of sense organs in the real time and space can it practically become the object to be interpreted. In other words, only when that object is sorted out into an objective form, namely ink and wash painting, can effective authentic knowledge be produced for the aesthetic cognition of members of the knowledge community. It may be proved from an opposite direction through ink and wash paintings that the object they try to convey is the congenital comprehensive ink and wash language, rather than the analytical artistic language. Yet a creative subject lacking congenital comprehensive ink and wash language can only get himself into a dead end by merely changing ways of producing paintings or trying to produce new variants (this is just the reason why people think incorrectly that the quality of one's ink and wash painting can be improved merely through efforts). In this case, the process of "finishing" an ink and wash painting is essentially that of producing a work of another genre — a substitutional form of ink and wash painting. As far as other genres of art such as oil painting, installation, project, video and media are concerned, the artist can acquire experience through practice, constantly revise the structure of his art form, and then expand his subjective aesthetic experience in turn. The creating subjects of these genres of art base their art on the analytical artistic language (as opposed to the congenital comprehensive language) that has innumerable ties with the material world.

Ink and wash painting creation is undoubtedly a kind of exploration of and research on, or more precisely, conjecture about, the existence (thing-in-itself) of the congenital comprehensive ink and wash language; it tries to reveal the fact of language about the inner world of the subject, known to neither others nor the subject himself: a fact that cannot be proved by practical experience. The creating subject tries to bring the congenital comprehensive ink and wash language to the bright world with introspective experience or introspective cognition and through the medium of ink and wash. Congenital comprehensive ink and wash language and ink and wash painting are two stages in the transition from the implicit to the explicit. The former is something before materialization, and the latter, after materialization. Due to its particularity, ink and wash painting is always in the process of presenting the ultimate state of congenital comprehensive ink and wash language and is the paradigms of the limited physical world. In any case, the result of creation is always limited and unreliable. All ink and wash paintings are knowledge form of a super-sensuous spiritual whole, and are attempts to explain the immeasurable spiritual whole with limited formal construction. The congenital comprehensive ink and wash language representing the inner sense of the individual are totally different from materials (for example, water, ink, paper and other mediums) embodying the universals. Therefore, the meaning of congenital comprehensive ink and wash language cannot be reduced to any definable form of meaning, and is not the sum of various forms of ink and wash painting, either. However, the congenital comprehensiveness of the tacit ink and wash language can be understood to some extent only when it is manifested as a concrete form of speech; it is in the logically paradoxical framework forever.

Therefore, we must also see that ink and wash painting is not so separated from congenital comprehensive ink and wash language as imagined. The task of ink and wash painting in decomposing the immeasurable and inexplicable congenital comprehensive whole into some single forms is to show how these single forms depend on the inner activities of the whole. As the external representation of the internal integral world, ink and wash painting is an incomplete mechanical existence. Being able to manifest ink and wash language in various forms, ink and wash paintings are various displays and contrasts of the inner world. Repeated creation of ink and wash paintings by the subject shows the yearning for inner spiritual integral world, thus mechanical forms and materials are used to explain the occurrences in the spiritual realm. The subject reduces spiritual things to material and tries to give impetus to the spirit of the whole natural system. In doing more ink and wash paintings, the subject attempts to offer more sufficient explanations for the whole natural system. In fact, the concrete actions of producing ink and wash paintings show the re-imaginations about and different views of the integral spiritual realm and make up for the deficiency of the mechanic nature of the ink and wash painting existing individually with changing and unstable states.

All congenitally comprehensive ink and wash languages are intrinsic nature of the subjects. Congenital comprehensive ink and wash languages have no necessary relationship with any explanations added to them: ink and wash paintings and critical theories about them. As stated above, congenital comprehensive ink and wash languages are originally tacit, and are un-explained system (whole). Explaining it in various ways using artificial language or symbols is a mistake of endowing something tacit an explicit speech. The mistake lies in the symbols already endowed with meaning being used to deduce meaning. Ink and wash painting, as a material form, is incorrectly supposed to be a copy of congenital comprehensive ink and wash language. In fact, the supposed form (ink and wash painting) is a simple and helpless understanding of the nature of spiritual language.

Ink and wash painting, once produced, will be activated again by aesthetic cognition, making it possible to generate more energy than that of itself which will act on the members of the knowledge community, including viewers, critics, the creator himself and other artists. Therefore, it is more appropriate to regard ink and wash painting as the logical effects of the ink and wash language, and the power of these effects originates from the congenital comprehensiveness of ink and wash language. The mistakes in the unavoidable contradictory problems may be reduced by constructing some finer systems through adding new symbols of various types, so that meanings in a wider range and more possibilities may be expressed and the relative value of ink and wash painting may be increased.

(Published originally in *Traditional Chinese Painter*, No. 4, 2000, Chinese Artists Association)

20世纪90年代
Works from the 1990s

胡志颖汇集了中国传统艺术与西方的折衷主义风格，以表现他所称的
"文化反差"。他将中国的传统象征手段和风景与西方艺术不同风格
的元素相结合，创造出不仅仅是艺术的事物——相当于现实世界的事
物。胡志颖使用了中国大漆、银粉、金粉与传统材料水墨、油彩和丙
烯，因此能够创造一种深入心灵的独特风格。

——亚当·唐纳德

Illustrating what he calls the "cultural contrast", Hu Zhiying brings together
traditional Chinese art with the eclectic styles of the West. He combines
traditional Chinese symbolism and landscape with the elements of the various
styles of Western art all coming together to create something more than art
— something equal to the real world. Using Chinese varnish, silver, and gold
powder with traditional ink, oils and acrylics, Hu Zhiying is able to create a
unique style that pierces into the soul.

— Adam Donald

红，1991，板上综合媒介，150×150cm
Red, 1991, mixed media on plank, 150 × 150 cm

红（局部）
Red (detail)

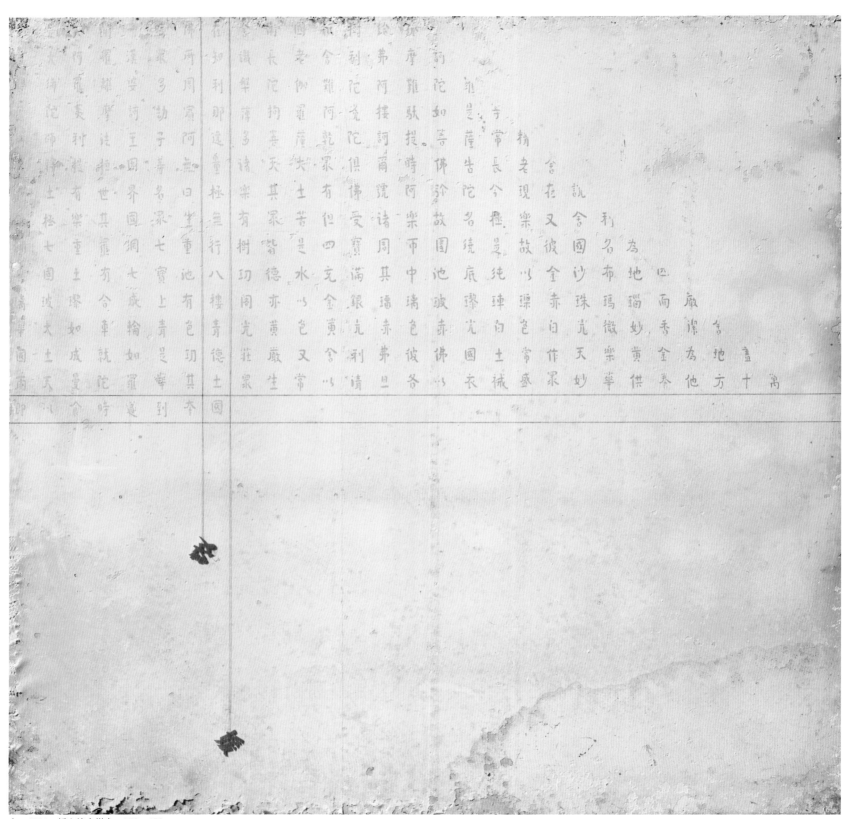

白，1991，板上综合媒介，150×150cm
White, 1991, mixed media on plank, 150 × 150 cm

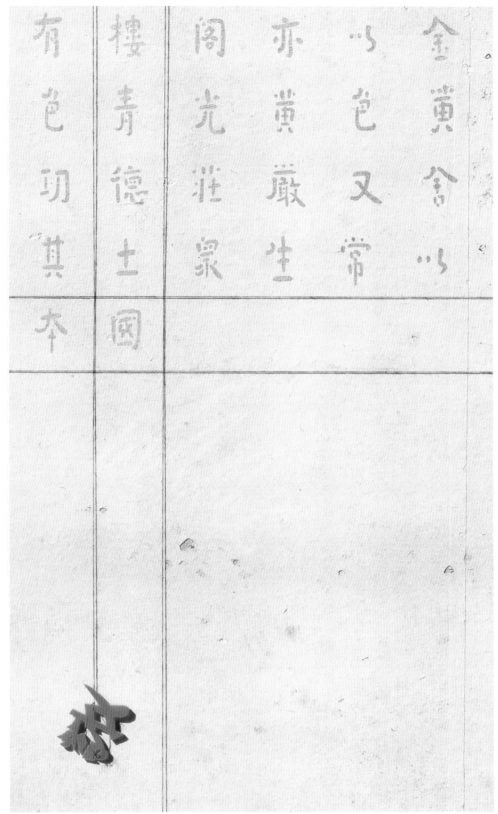

金黄谷以

以色又常

亦黄嚴生

閣光莊衆

樓青德士國

有色功其本

白（局部）
White (detail)

黑，1991，板上综合媒介，150×150cm
Black, 1991, mixed media on plank, 150 × 150 cm

黑（局部）
Black (detail)

文字之一，1992，布上综合媒介，180×200cm
Characters I, 1992, mixed media on canvas, 180 × 200 cm

文字之二，1992，布上综合媒介，180×200cm
Characters II, 1992, mixed media on canvas, 180 × 200 cm

文字之二（局部）
Characters II (detail)

文字之三，1992，布上综合媒介，180×200cm
Characters III, 1992, mixed media on canvas, 180 × 200 cm

胡志颖的作品均为综合材料，材料的具象性正是在它自身与其所负载的艺术含义之间，脱离直接关联的变异中失却其具象性质，而受限于艺术的自律性。媒介材料的具体物质性与其在艺术作品中所呈现的抽象性之间又产生一种悬隔。是靠作为与现实世界等量齐观的艺术现实本身还是靠对现实世界的诠释，恐怕是难以解决的，也许这是不必纠缠的一个形而上问题，切入其语言言说的句词之中进行分辨也许是最终的目的。

——《中国当代美术家图鉴》

Mixed media is used in Hu Zhiying's works without exception. The lack of direct link between the materials and the artistic meanings they carry deprives the materials of their figurative nature and subjects them to the autonomy of art. A gap arises between the concrete materiality of the materials and the abstractness they manifest in works of art. It is difficult, I am afraid, to decide whether we should base our understanding on the artistic reality itself on a par with the real world or on the explanation of the real world. Perhaps this is a metaphysical problem unnecessary for us to be involved in. Maybe our final aim is to analyse the context of the artistic language.

— A Pictorial book of Contemporary Chinese Artists

文字之三（局部）
Characters III (detail)

文字之五，1992，板上综合媒介，200 × 180cm
Characters V, 1992, mixed media on plank, 200 × 180 cm

阅读胡志颖的作品给人一种东方虚化境界的感受，而他对整个画面的光滑的处理又提醒我们面对一个物质的实存空间。画布、画板以及材料的色彩、形态、质感把我们所体验到的虚化境界悬隔在物质空间之外。

——赵　冰

When beholding Hu Zhiying's work, we are impressed by its etherealness peculiar to Oriental Art, while we are reminded by the smooth effect of the whole painting that we are confronted with a substantial space. The canvas, the panel and the colors, forms and textures of materials exclude the etherealness we have sensed from the material space.

— Zhao Bing

文字之五（局部）
Characters V (detail)

文字之六，1992，板上综合媒介，200×180cm
Characters VI, 1992, mixed media on plank, 200 × 180 cm

胡志颖运用中国传统题材，并以难以想象的特殊技巧将耀眼的红色和黄色恰如其分地协调在巨幅画面上。其艺术是通过多元美学观念直率地阐说画中的象征意义。

——巴巴拉·罗曼

Hu Zhiying uses traditional subject matters of China and harmonizes dazzling red and yellow appropriately on his huge paintings with an unimaginable special technique. His art lies in the straightforward expounding of the symbolic meanings in his paintings through diversified aesthetic concepts.

— Barbara Rollmann

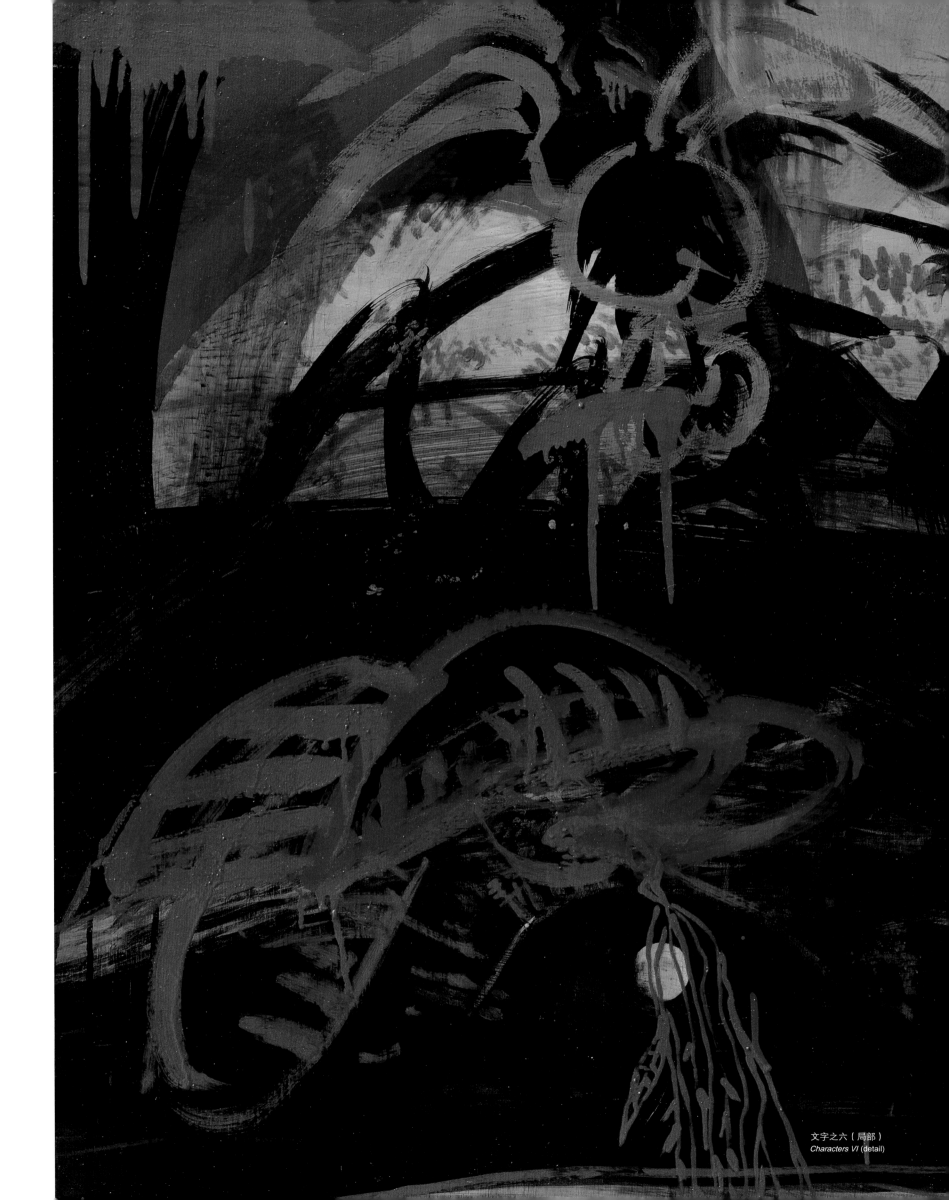

文字之六（局部）
Characters VI (detail)

我在整张画做了一层水墨底子或单色底子后，用中国大漆罩一遍，使整个画面处于一种深色略偏褐色的氛围中。然后我选择既与底子的图像不同文化元素、又在视觉上形成一定程度反差而又能相互依存的造型。画面不同层次的融洽和交织倚仗于绘画性很强的技术语言。材料的使用也是东西方不同材质的并举——大漆、砥砆与油彩、丙烯综合为一种不同寻常的迷离效果。

——胡志颖

After doing a layer of ink and wash underpainting or homochromatic underpainting on the whole surface, I cover it with Chinese lacquer so that the whole surface is enveloped in a dark brownish atmosphere. Then I choose some shapes that have different cultural elements from the under painting and that can form a contrast with each other visually to some extent and can also interdepend. Harmony and interweavement of different elements at various levels in my works depends on powerful technical language of painting. The materials I use also embody the combination of the East and the West: Chinese lacquer, vermilion, oil paint and acrylic are used simultaneously, achieving an unusual and vague effect.

— Hu Zhiying

数学之一，1994，板上综合媒介，180×200cm
Mathematics I, 1994, mixed media on plank,180 × 200 cm

数学之二，1994，板上综合媒介，180×200cm
Mathematics II, 1994, mixed media on plank, 180 × 200 cm

数学之二（局部）
Mathematics II (detail)

在对中国传统艺术进行深入研究学习和对西方艺术史上的抽象表现主义模仿、现成品艺术试验和制作之后，我又重新开始画画。目的在对过去二十年，我一直在探索的一个我称之为"文化反差"的问题，作更广阔意义上的进一步探究。我在创作笔记中写道："我在我的作品中常常综合中国绘画中的符号和西方绘画产生的隐在的折衷主义的文化价值。"我将中国传统山水画混合于变化的各种西方风格元素之中。我喜欢把我的作品等同于真实世界，而不只是它的一个文本。我的画频繁地合成多种物象的想象，这些物象致使背景与前景经常发生交互性变化。

——胡志颖

After making a penetrating study of traditional Chinese art, imitating abstract expressionism in Western art history and experimenting on ready-made art, I began to produce paintings again with the purpose of making a further inquiry in a wider sense into what I call "cultural contrast", a problem I have been exploring in the past two decades. I write in my note on artistic creation, " I often incorporate the signs from Chinese painting and latent eclectic cultural values derived from Western painting in my works." I often mix Chinese traditional landscape painting with various changed elements of Western styles. I like to identify my works with the real world rather than mere texts about it. Imaginations about varied images are frequently composed in my paintings, and these images lead to frequent reciprocal change between the background and the foreground.

— Hu Zhiying

数学之三，1994，布上综合媒介，200×173cm
Mathematics III, 1994, mixed media on canvas, 200 × 173 cm

数学之四，1994，布上综合媒介，200×173cm
Mathematics IV, 1994, mixed media on canvas, 200 × 173 cm

天文之二，1995，板上综合媒介，200×180cm
Astronomy II, 1995, mixed media on plank, 200 × 180 cm

胡志颖的艺术把经典的传统西方艺术如塞尚和诸如安塞尔·亚当斯这种西方现代摄影巧妙地交织于经典的中国艺术形式之中。

——冯·彼得·米夏茨克

Hu Zhiying's art skillfully interweaves classical and traditional Western art such as Cezanne's and Western modern photography such as Ansel Adams's with classical Chinese art form.

— Von Peter Michalzik

天文之一，1995，布上综合媒介，180×200cm
Astronomy I, 1995, mixed media on plank, 180 × 200 cm

天文之一（局部）
Astronomy I (detail)

天文之三，1995，板上综合媒介，180×200cm
Astronomy III, 1995, mixed media on plank, 180 × 200 cm

天文之三（局部）
Astronomy III (detail)

方程式之一，1996，布上综合媒介，200 × 180cm
Equations I, 1996, mixed media on canvas, 200 × 180 cm

方程式之一（局部）
Equations I (detail)

胡志颖的画面运用金粉、银粉和中国大漆形成闪光的效果，而这种效果在中国艺术中是最容易引起争议的。但这正是他艺术之所在：利用外来文化同时又瓦解它使之渗透到自己的传统之中。

——萨比内·阿德勒

The use of gold powder, silver powder and Chinese lacquer in Hu Zhiying's paintings brings about a shining effect, an effect easiest to arouse controversy in Chinese art. However, this is exactly where his art lies: making use of foreign cultures but at the same time disintegrating them and incorporating them into his own tradition.

— Sabine Adler

胡志颖的作品，有很多空间的叠合，有中国的空间感，也有西画的元素，画面趣味很复杂、难以言表，在画面营造多重意思。
——高　岭

There are overlaps of space in Hu Zhiying's works. There is sense of space peculiar to Chinese art and also elements of Western painting. His paintings have indescribable and complex taste, and multiple meanings are created in them.

— Gao Ling

方程式之二，1996，布上综合媒介，180×200cm
Equations II, 1996, mixed media on canvas, 180 × 200 cm

方程式之二（局部）
Equations II (detail)

方程式之三，1996，布上综合媒介，200×180cm
Equations III, 1996, mixed media on canvas, 200 × 180 cm

在胡志颖的作品中，我们似乎感到他个人文化影像的一层层剥离和呈现、一次次拆解和重组，而同时，这种文化影像却又不仅仅是个人的意义，而是一次次地指向更广阔的地域和文化空间，对重大的文化构成提出既具有理性又充满激情的质疑。

——王璜生

It seems that we can sense, in Hu Zhiying's works, the peeling off and representing, layer after layer, and disassembling and regrouping, time and again, of his personal cultural images. While at the same time, these cultural images not only have personal significance, but also point to a wider area and cultural space, raising questions full of reason and will about significant cultural constructions.

— Wang Huangsheng

方程式之三（局部）
Equations III (detail)

方程式之四，1996，布上综合媒介，180×200cm
Equations IV, 1996, mixed media on canvas, 180 × 200 cm

胡志颖的绘画方式是解构中西方艺术的不同元素而后综合之。胡志颖用西方的材料表现中国艺术的因素并体现饶有个性的平整的表面效果，从而使其艺术富于复合的现代意义。

——英格·林德曼

Hu Zhiying's mode of painting lies in the disintegrating and subsequent integrating of different elements of Chinese and Western art. Hu Zhiying expresses elements of Chinese art with Western materials and enhances the distinct flat effect of the painting surface so that his art is full of multiple modern meanings.

— Inge Lindemann

方程式之四（局部）
Equations IV (detail)

胡志颖的作品的意义不仅仅是对中西方艺术的融合，他对经典艺术的引用不是简单的引用，更重要的是对经典的东西方艺术（包括传统和现代）的重构，即在东方和西方的伟大艺术成就基础上重造艺术，创造出属于他自己的艺术。

——青　宇

The significance of Hu Zhiying's art lies not only in his combination of Chinese and Western art. He does not make use of classical art in a simple way. What is more important is the reconstruction of classical Eastern and Western art (including traditional and modern), i.e., he reshapes art on the basis of the great artistic achievements of the East and the West and creates his own art.

— Qing Yu

方程式之五，1996，布上综合媒介，180×200cm
Equations V, 1996, mixed media on canvas, 180 × 200 cm

方程式之五（局部）
Equations V (detail)

原子之一，1997，布上综合媒介，200 × 180cm
Atoms I, 1997, mixed media on canvas, 200 × 180 cm

胡志颖正是重视于意识的过程，以意识的过程来表述文化的状态。于是，在他的画面，意识一层层地展开，文化的影像层叠显现出来，追问、怀疑、撞击成了文化意识本身。

——王璜生

Hu Zhiying attaches importance to the process of consciousness and represents the state of culture through it. So in his paintings, consciousness is unfolded layer after layer and cultural images are displayed one after another; questioning, suspecting and colliding become the cultural consciousness itself.

— Wang Huangsheng

原子之一（局部）
Atoms I (detail)

胡志颖的画面常常是多种物象的综合，作为物象的背景与背景中的物象往往交替互换。胡志颖的作品真正例示了他所谓的"文化反差"具体而又抽象的感知范围，当人们意欲追溯这种感知范围的历史原型时，当人们意欲追究其母题与主题的联系时，却又很容易陷入画中不可名状的虚化的梦境之中。其作品中呈现的那些具体物质材料把一种古典色调与多元并置的图象所表现的文化反差置于精致的物质性感受当中，从而体验其多种悬隔感。复杂的材料、变幻的图象、光洁如镜的表面与我们身处其中瞬息万变、充满奇光异彩的世界正相暗合，而从浮光之下又透出与此相隔的幽冥神秘的境界。

——《十五位中国当代艺术家工作室》

Hu Zhiying's pictures are often a synthesis of many different types of objects, and the background as images and the images in the foreground tend to replace each other. Hu Zhiying's works illustrate "cultural contrast" as an abstract and concrete field of knowledge. When the viewer tries to discern the origin of this field and identify the relationship between the themes of art and their prototypes, they are likely to lose themselves in the dreamlike realm of the paintings. In his easel paintings on canvas or board, apart from conventional materials like ink, oil and acrylic colors, Hu Zhiying applies gold and silver power as well as Chinese lacquer. The various materials, the diversity of images and the glossy surface are easily identifiable with the bright yet unstable reality of the world in which we live, and at the same time, imply a dark, mysterious world lurking beneath the dazzling surface.

— *China-Aktuelles aus 15 Ateliers*

原子之二，1997，布上综合媒介，180×200cm
Atoms II, 1997, mixed media on canvas, 180 × 200 cm

原子之二（局部）
Atoms II (detail)

原子之三，1997，布上综合媒介，180×200cm
Atoms III, 1997, mixed media on canvas, 180 × 200 cm

西方的超现实主义传统，把人的创造力放在一种没有约束的境域，强调一种绝对的创造力，而不是一种相对的创造力，我在胡志颖的作品中看到了这样一种东西。加上他画面空间上的错置，它既非透视的也非故意反透视法的，实际上是没有一个固定视点的，他不是为了刻画什么、再现什么、或者主观意义上表达什么，绘画对他而言实际上是一种探寻的过程，在这种过程，才利用了一些符号。我特别感兴趣的是他运用材料的讲究，从材料上来看，他喜欢用大漆、砥砥，这让我想起中国汉代的漆艺，具有一种历史的深度，漆的多层效果给人一种肃穆、凝固的感觉。

——鲍　栋

In Western surrealist tradition, the human creativity is free from any restraint, and absolute rather than relative creativity is emphasized. Such is the thing that I have sensed in Hu Zhiying's works. With dislocation of things in the space, his paintings are something that neither conforms to perspective nor goes against it intentionally. In fact, there is not a fixed point of view. He does not portray or represent anything, or express anything in subjective sense. For him, painting is in fact a process of exploration, and signs are made use of in this process. I am particularly interested in his exquisite use of materials. In terms of materials, he likes to use lacquer and vermilion which remind me of the lacquer art of the Han Dynasty in China. They have a historical depth. The effect of multi-layered lacquer strikes one as solemn and solidified.

— Bao Dong

原子之三（局部）
Atoms III (detail)

原子之四，1997，布上综合媒介，200 × 180cm
Atoms IV, 1997, mixed media on canvas, 200 × 180 cm

我无法抑制地需要某些特别的方式表达自己，因而我就无法固定某一种模式或固守某种不变的风格。甚至我需要用互为冲突的创作过程和迥然不同的视觉刺激来满足我的这一需要。惟有两种或多种强烈反差的情绪和思维活动所形成的广阔巨大的空间方能满足我的这一需要。我一直以来都倾心于我以为十分重要的"文化反差"，因而我的作品常常出现东西方不同元素的交织，通过多种材料甚至综合媒介来表达这一反差，最终的效果却又皈依于单纯。

——胡志颖

I need uncontrollably some special modes to express myself; therefore I cannot fix a certain mode or cling to some unchanged style. I even have to satisfy this need of mine with mutually conflicting processes of creation and utterly different visual stimuli. Only the vast and enormous space formed by two or more kinds of sharply contrastive moods and thinking activities can satisfy this need of mine. I have been engrossed all along in the "cultural contrast" which I think very important, and therefore interweavement of different elements of the East and the West often appear in my works. I try to express this contrast through various materials and even mixed media but the final effect remains simple.

— Hu Zhiying

原子之四（局部）
Atoms IV (detail)

原子之五，1997，布上丙烯，水墨，大漆，180×200cm
Atoms V, 1997, acrylic, ink and lacquer on canvas, 180 × 200 cm

内典录之一，1997–1998，绢上丙烯，墨，木炭，195×183cm
Buddhist Scriptures I, 1997-1998, acrylic, ink and charcoal on silk, 195 × 183 cm

中国的胡志颖也展示了一件题为《内典录之一》的强烈而富有气势的作品。画中运用了绢本水墨的古典媒材和亚
洲传统山水画卷流畅而繁复的线条来表现一种完全当代的、极具想象力的艺术感觉，以创造充满着令人震撼的意
象的混茫原始的自然奇观。

———莫里斯·塔普林格

China's Hu Zhiying also makes a strong showing with a work entitled *Buddhist Scriptures I*, in which the ancient medium
of ink on silk and the linear fluidity and intricacy of traditional Asian landscape scrolls are put to the service of a thoroughly
contemporary, highly imaginative artistic sensibility to create starling primordial nature fantasies filled with electrifying imagery.

— Maurice Taplinger

佛典录之一（局部一）
Buddhist Scriptures 1 (detail 1)

在他的《内典录之一》中，胡志颖用绢上丙烯、墨和木炭，创建了一个不祥、恐怖和美的深邃世界。《内典录之一》令人联想起他的带有攀援的"藤蔓"和风景风格的《天文之一》和《天文之三》，看上去像我们日常所见事物的神秘的底侧。在这幅画中，胡志颖向我们表明了他的文化反差——光明的世界与既可与生活并立同样也可与艺术并立的神秘的彼岸世界。

——亚当·唐纳德

In his *Buddhist Scriptures I* Zhiying, using acrylic, ink and charcoal on silk, creates a depth that is ominous, forbidding, and beautiful. Reminiscent of his *Astronomy I* and *III* with the climbing "vines" and landscape style, *Buddhist Scriptures I* looks like the mysterious underside of what we see everyday. In this painting Zhiying shows us his cultural contrast — the bright world with the mysterious other side that can stand along side life and art equally.

内典录之一（局部二）
Buddhist Scriptures I (detail 2)

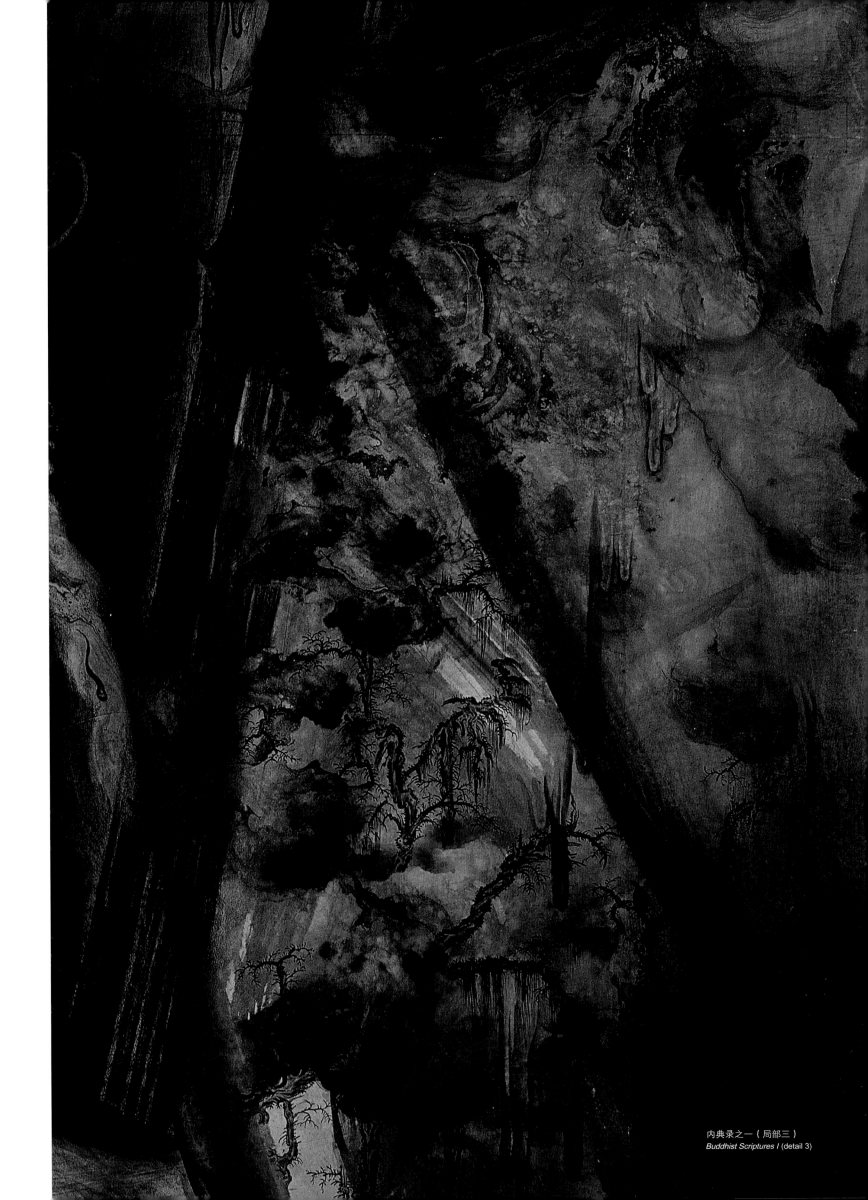

内典录之一（局部三）
Buddhist Scriptures I (detail 3)

内典录之二，1997–1998，绢上丙烯，墨，木炭，183×195cm
Buddhist Scriptures II, 1997-1998, acrylic, ink and charcoal on silk, 183 × 195 cm

艺术原本就不是一种固定不变的东西，即使面对同一件艺术作品，也有可能发生种种不同个体的感受或认知，因而我们无法找到它的唯一真相。而渗透着强烈主观因素的当代艺术更难以达到还原其真相的描述或阐述，这正是当代艺术的多元化以及不确定性的魅力所在。

——胡志颖

Art is never something changeless. We are unable to find its only truth, for one same work of art may arouse different impressions or understandings in different individuals. It is still more difficult to achieve a depiction or exposition of contemporary art, permeated with strongly subjective elements, able to lead back to the truth. This is exactly where the glamour of the diversity and uncertainty of contemporary art lies.

— Hu Zhiying

内典录之二（局部一）
Buddhist Scriptures II (detail 1)

内典录之二（局部 二）
Buddhist Scriptures II (detail 2)

内典录之二（局部三）
Buddhist Scriptures II (detail 3)

内典录之三，1997–1998，绢上丙烯，墨，木炭，183×195cm
Buddhist Scriptures III, 1997-1998, acrylic, ink and charcoal on silk, 183 × 195 cm

内典录之三（局部一）
Buddhist Scriptures III (detail 1)

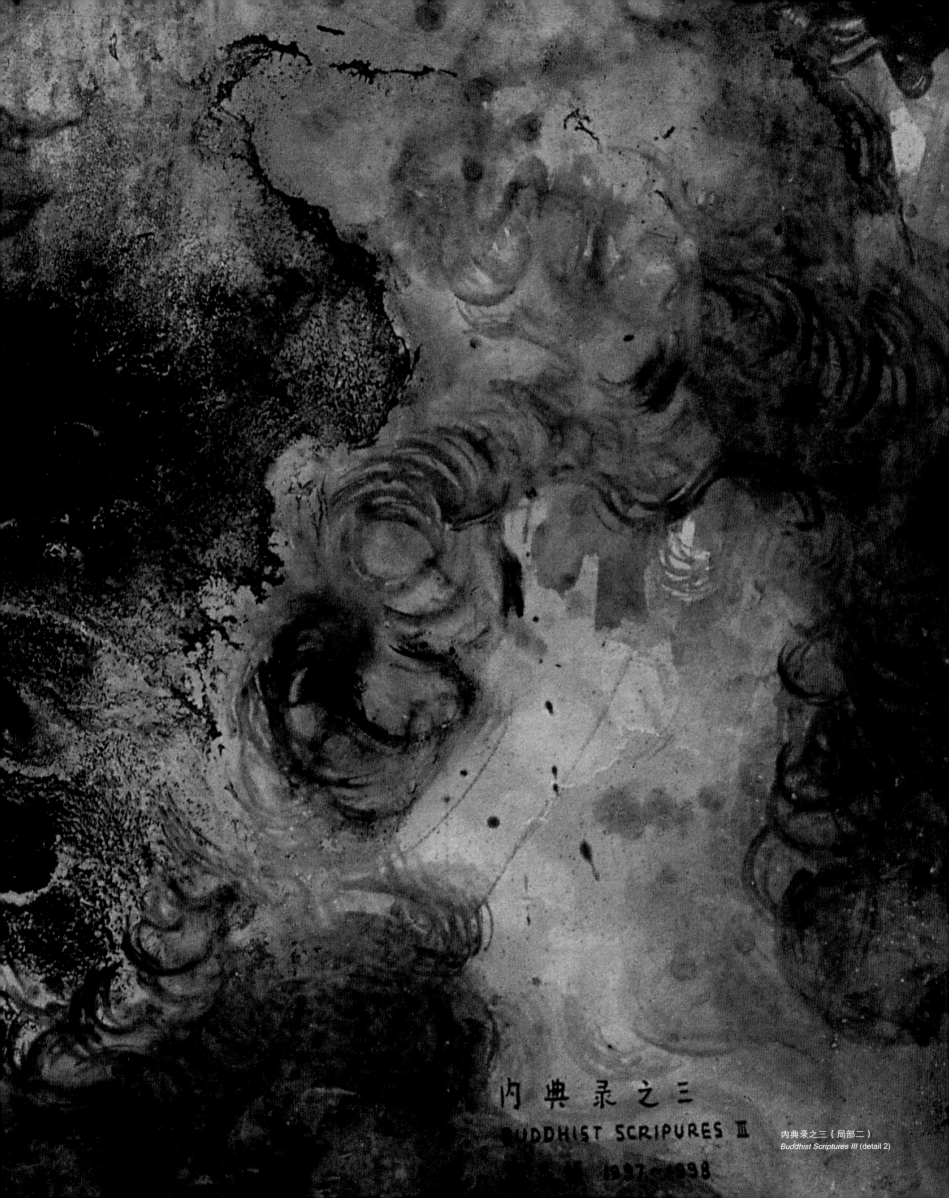

内典录之三

BUDDHIST SCRIPURES III

内典录之三（局部二）
Buddhist Scriptures III (detail 2)

内典录之四，1997–1998，绢上丙烯，墨，木炭，195×183cm
Buddhist Scriptures IV, 1997-1998, acrylic, ink and charcoal on silk, 195 × 183 cm

胡志颖这些山水，很奇异，很怪诞，很斑斓，而且很神秘，气象很大。跟东方的语境和我们传统的文脉有关系，而
且，在里面又强化了它的形而上。

——杨 卫

These landscapes by Hu Zhiying are very unusual, weird, gorgeous, mysterious and magnificent. They have something to do with
the Eastern context and our tradition, and metaphysical elements are enhanced in them.

— Yang Wei

内典录之四（局部一）
Buddhist Scriptures IV (detail 1)

内典录之四（局部二）
Buddhist Scriptures IV (detail 2)

我极为欣赏胡志颖的《内典录》。它们呈现了艺术家的智慧并且展示了他自己个性化的视觉想象力和语言表现力。他的表达极其富有力量并傲然独立。

——威廉·J. 希伊

I enjoy Hu Zhiying's *Buddhist Scriptures* the most. They showcase his facility and also show off his own personal vision and voice. His voice is very powerful and can stand alone.

— William J. Sheehy

内典录之五，1999–2003，绢上丙烯，墨，木炭，植物颜料，183×195cm
Buddhist Scriptures V, 1999-2003, acrylic, ink, charcoal and plant pigment on silk, 183 × 195 cm

内典录之五（局部一）
Buddhist Scriptures V (detail 1)

内典录之五（局部二）
Buddhist Scriptures V (detail 2)

正是因为胡志颖的这种不懈探索精神，驱使他一次次地超越自我，将自己的绘画艺术不断引向历史的纵深，到后来与更大的文化背景联系在了一起。这可以理解为胡志颖对现实世界的超越，已经不再是简单地关心现实问题，而是遨游于浩瀚汪洋的历史大海，将自我的现实纳入到了文化传统的悠悠长河之中。

──杨　卫

It is this spirit of persevering exploration that makes Hu Zhiying surpass himself again and again and bring his art of painting to the depth of history continuously so that it is connected with the larger cultural background afterwards. It can be understood in this way: his transcendence of the real world no longer lies in merely concerning himself with practical problems; instead, he now swims in the boundless sea of history, bringing his own personal reality into the long river of cultural tradition.

— Yang Wei

内典录之六，1999–2003，绢上丙烯，墨，木炭，植物颜料，195×183cm
Buddhist Scriptures VI, 1999-2003, acrylic, ink, charcoal and plant pigment on silk, 195 × 183 cm

内典录之六（局部）
Buddhist Scriptures VI (detail)

内典录之七，1999–2003，绢上丙烯，墨，木炭，油画棒，植物颜料，195×183cm
Buddhist Scriptures VII, 1999-2003, acrylic, ink, charcoal,oil crayon and plant pigment on silk, 195 × 183 cm

内典录之七（局部一）
Buddhist Scriptures VII (detail 1)

《在幻象锁链的彼岸》是法兰克福学派哲学家艾里克·弗洛姆的著作，在这本书中，他把弗洛伊德的无意识学说与马克思的意识形态学说联系起来，重新反思了人类自由的可能性。在这里，我们借用这本书的标题来概括胡志颖的绘画语言与艺术境界：通过一系列的视觉符号、形象及象征的可见的"链条"来抵达某种不可见的实体，一种无法被文化所定义，无法由经验所感知，亦不可被语言所触及的存在本真。

——鲍　栋

Beyond the Chains of Illusion is a work of Erich Fromm, a philosopher of Frankfurt School. In this book, the author connected the theory of Unconsciousness by Freud and the ideological theory of Marx, re-reflected the possibility of human freedom. Here, we conclude Hu Zhiying's painting language and art realm with the title of this book: to reach some invisible substance through the visible "chains" of a series of visual symbols, images and indications, which is the authenticity of existence that cannot be defined by culture, perceived by experience or touched by language.

--- Bao Dong

内典录之七（局部二）
Buddhist Scriptures VII (detail 2)

内典录之八，1999–2003，绢上丙烯，墨，木炭，植物颜料，183×195cm
Buddhist Scriptures VIII, 1999-2003, acrylic, ink, charcoal and plant pigment on silk, 183 × 195 cm

总体而言，我希望既确立一种艺术形式完璧无瑕的统一，又在其中肯定自然宇宙存在的矛盾与协调的无穷变化；既溶解理智的坚冰，又平息激情的喷薄；而以自然宿命和人为秩序统一内心深处无以名状的灵魂语言，获得既稳定永恒，又给幻想玄思以极大空间的表达方式。

——胡志颖

Generally speaking, I hope both to establish a perfect unity of forms of art and affirm the infinite changes of contradictions and harmonies existing in natural universe; both to melt the hard ice of reason and subside the outburst of passion; to unify the language of the soul beyond description in the depth of human mind with natural fatalism and man-made order and obtain a stable and eternal mode of expression that will provide enormous space for illusion and fantasy.

— Hu Zhiying

内典录之八（局部一）
Buddhist Scriptures VIII (detail 1)

内典录之八（局部二）
Buddhist Scriptures VIII (detail 2)

胡志颖的《内典录》有东方与自己的精神分析在里面，既是突破水墨的窠臼，也是当代中的一种冒险。
——王春辰

Hu Zhiying's *Buddhist Scriptures*, with Oriental elements and Hu's own psychoanalysis in it, has broken with old patterns of ink and wash and is at the same time an adventure in the contemporary era.

— Wang Chunchen

内典录之八（局部三）
Buddhist Scriptures VIII (detail 3)

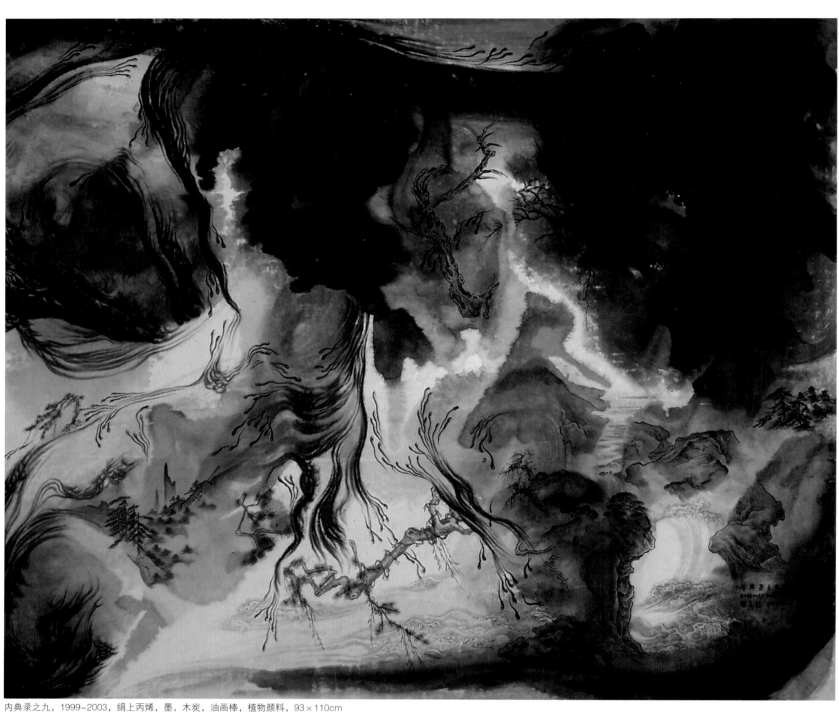

内典录之九，1999–2003，绢上丙烯，墨，木炭，油画棒，植物颜料，93×110cm
Buddhist Scriptures IX, 1999-2003, acrylic, ink, charcoal, oil crayon and plant pigment on silk, 93 × 110 cm

内典录之十，1999–2003，绢上丙烯，墨，木炭，油画棒，植物颜料，93×110cm
Buddhist Scriptures X, 1999-2003, acrylic, ink, charcoal, oil crayon and plant pigment on silk, 93 × 110 cm

文化权力的无常

——解读胡志颖

王璜生

在我们这个社会和年代，脑袋里、眼睛里装满了种种文化的影像。公共的、私密的、东方的、西方的、古典的、现代的……彼此交叉缠绕，构成一种独特而庞杂的文化图像，每个人都以自己独特的方式来吸摄和重组这样一些图像，并构成每个人自身的"文化概念"和"文化权力"。每个人似乎可以理直气壮地去述说作为文化的意义，但同时，每个人却又发现自己的"文化"无可依归，不知自己的"文化图像"符号落实在何处，不知何为自己的图像基础，何为外来强行进入的符号因素。多重的文化符号本身正构成一种独特的符号文化。因此，艺术家自觉而敏感地对这种符号文化以体验、感觉和表现，而同时，艺术家自身所具备的理性精神和权力意志却常常对这种文化提出疑问、对这种文化的基础及存在的合理性发出追问。胡志颖正是属于这种敏于感觉又善于追问的艺术家。正因为他敏于感觉，因此在他的艺术表现中呈现为多元且庞杂的视觉影像，使我们似乎在一种无序和对抗中感受到生命的茫然和丰富，仿佛在一个无限的时空中穿梭与碰撞，一片诱惑的红色像巨大能量的旋涡令无常的生命如蜉蝣一样眩转。意识跳跃般的闪亮；另一方面，又因为他善于追问，因而在这穿越时空的茫然眩转中，我们感觉到一种理性力量的存在，追问一种文化的存在与构成，有如追问生命存在的意义和价值，尤其是在无序的文化状态中，这种追问更需要一种意志的力量，用意志去叩问无常。

于是，胡志颖因一篇鸿论《艺术无常论》惹起了一场风波，个人的思考和表达成了对所谓权威的挑战。如果说意志和性格能够战胜世俗和名利欲望，能够战胜自我的生命懦弱，但，它却无法面对代表着"文化"的权力和权威，因为权力有权不与他面对面，不与他争论。福柯认为，话语和权力联结在一起，没有权力也就构不成话语，没有话语也等于没有了权力。这正应验于胡志颖的论点：艺术无常、文化无常，那么，权力有常吗？

文化的主要问题是权力问题，从大的空间讲，以西方为权力中心的"西方文化主义"和东方被迫抵制意志和附和潜意识的"东方主义"，构成了一个权力重新分配及碰撞、抗争、消解的局面，不同的文化在这其中所呈现出来的话语因素及趋向，其潜台词和潜在的可能性始终联结着出席权和在场权问题。而对同一个文化问题的提出和接受，如"认同与差异"（"第46届威尼斯双年展"的主题），东西方都以自己的权力话语进行着各自的表达，并在表达中尽可能争取着权力的体现。而作为区域、群组、个人，这种文化的权力构成及存在也同样是暴露性和侵犯性的，各自都在争取发言的权利，而彼此的发言却相互干扰、相互抵消；各自都在争取和构成自己的文化权力，但却发现自己的文化权力在众多他人的文化权力中显得微不足道以至于彼此消解，并且往往被超越文化之外的权力所侵犯和践踏。这一切都似乎包孕着最深层的无奈，而更无奈的还在于个体心理所构成的文化堡垒彼此的独立、冲撞、无法沟通和无可奈何。作为艺术家，只能在感觉和表现的可能范围和权力许可中来思考和发问这并置、冲撞、消解的文化心理问题。

因此，在胡志颖的作品中，我们似乎感觉到他个人文化影像的一层层剥离和呈现、一次次拆解和重组，而同时，这种文化影像却不仅仅是个人的意义，而是一次次地指向更广阔的地域和文化空间，对重大的文化构成提出充满理性和意志的质疑。

可以看到，对古典的宋画、对狂野的民间艺术、对水墨表现性的独特感觉，以及蕴涵理性的张力，这构成了胡志颖个人文化影像的基础。从他早期的种种作品（图1，2，3）以及他对书法和水墨抽象的兴趣，我们似乎可以为他的图像脉络理出一些依据。在他近期的作品中，经常出现一些南宋山水符号，甚至很明确的马远《踏歌图》符号，还有红、黑、金、银的民间色彩构成和民间髹漆原料，以及笔墨表现性很强的局部抽象元素，由此我们也许可以轻易地将之归类为东方式的文化影像。但是问题并非如此简单和清晰，当我们认可于某种东西，甚至希冀以某种东西为基础以吸纳重组时，也许我们碰到的最大难题是对这种基础的怀疑，我们的吸纳和重组在这种怀疑中变得犹豫不定且无所适从。这也许是一种意识过程，也是文化发生和发展的过程。胡志颖正是重视了意识的过程，以意识的过程来表述文化的状态。于是，在他的画面，意识一层层地展开，文化的影像层叠显现出来，追问、怀疑、撞击成了文化意识本身。从他的画面，我们似乎感觉到一种对现代艺术之父塞尚的怀疑而崇敬的态度；对时空意识瓦解的关注和幽冥神秘境界的眷恋；对宗教感的怀念和消解；对心理空间的跨越和冻结；对生命本身的热情熔铸和理性剖析……胡志颖正是企图以这种文化影像的多重性构筑它们新一层的意义。如果说，作为艺术家的胡志颖以文化的并置和撞击过程完成他作为艺术家的表现意义的话，那么，作为理性沉思者的胡志颖却以这里为起点，进一步追问和怀疑文化的权力问题，而他的结论却落实在"无常"上：我们无法分清宋代艺术在当代中国生活关系中潜在的意义及权力指向的能量，以及这种指向和能量与现代或后现代艺术之间在当代社会中构成的文化关系；我们无法面对"踏歌"式田园牧歌的精神向往与暴力恐惧潜伏的欲望激刺并置于一个共同的心理空间；我们无法在一种红色的狂热和世俗的煽情中接受一种墨色的宗教冥思……在这里，作为个人的文化权力和作为社会、公众的文化权力既互相对抗、冲突又时而合谋、消解，当我们自认获得一种文化权力和话语方式并进行个人的发言时，其终了却无奈地发现自己的话语其实是他人的话语所暗示（侵犯）的结果，自己的所谓权力往往是他人权力武器中的一个小齿轮，它无奈地被动地运转着。这也许就是胡志颖企图对以权力为支点的文化所做的怀疑和追问，追问的结果却是无奈的。于是，他只能为自己的一系列作品安上一系列无奈的标题："五·一 己巳6·9 五·十一 己卯6·19 五·二十一 己丑6·29"、"九·一 癸卯10·20 九·十一 癸丑10·30 九·二十一 癸亥11·9"、"周贞定王元年癸酉（公元前468年）"等等，这些与画面似乎无任何联系的标题，你完全可以怀疑其用意和其意义，而这种怀疑正是胡志颖的用意和意义之所在。

毕竟，胡志颖是艺术家，艺术家的许多工作是落实在具体的甚至是工匠式的技术操作层面上的。没有这种技术操作和技术难度，任何意义的怀疑和

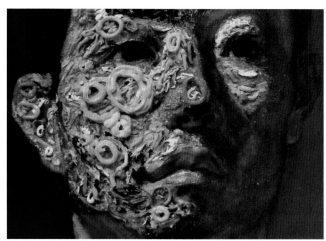

（图1）自画像（局部），1990-1991，布上油彩、蛋胶，110×110cm
(Fig. 1) *Self-portrait (detail)*, 1990-1991, oil and tempuras on canvas, 110 × 110 cm

（图2）拼贴（局部，已毁），1990-1991，布上综合媒介，110×110cm
(Fig. 2) *Collage (detail, destroyed)*, 1990-1991, mixed media on canvas, 110 × 110 cm

（图3）作品14号（已毁），1990，板上油彩、油漆，200×400cm
(Fig. 3) *Works No.14 (destroyed)*, 1990, oil and paint on plank, 200 × 400 cm

追问将是一团迷雾状的空想。尽管，胡志颖对外部空间的文化权力有着无奈的感觉，但，他却对自己艺术所应具有的权力意志十分明确。也就是说，他对自己的艺术语言有着明确的建构指向，他选择工艺技术性极强的髹漆手艺来切入当代文化表现和思考，注重甚至可称考究于色彩、材料（包括画布、木板、阳江漆、大漆、金银粉箔、砇碟等等）以及画面符号、线条、块面的可欣赏性，以此来建构他的艺术话语的堡垒。

当然，我这样解读胡志颖，对于他人来说未必有意义，对于胡本人来说，也同样可能是文化权力侵犯的结果，这正是当代文化的无奈。我以我的文化权力言说一种艺术存在和现象，而胡志颖和他者，也同样以其各自的文化意志构建各自的文化堡垒。在一个貌似开放且信息覆盖强度空前的后现代社会，解构成了一种时髦和必然的选择，但解构并不是拆除堡垒之墙，而是各自在滥用和加强自己的文化权力，以之侵犯和消解他人的权力，而彼此的加强和消解、权力的聚集和抵消，这正是当代世界文化范围内的必然趋势。

（原载《江苏画刊》1997年第二期，江苏美术出版社）

The Transiency of Cultural Power

— Reading Hu Zhiying

By Wang Huangsheng

In our age and society, our minds and eyes are filled with various cultural images. Public, private; east, west; classical, modern…They intersect each other and intertwine together, constituting a kind of unique, numerous and jumbled cultural images. Everyone absorbs and regroups these images in his own unique way and constructs "cultural concept" and "cultural power" of his own. It seems that everyone can give an account of the significance of culture with perfect assurance, yet at the same time, everyone finds that it is difficult to decide what category his "culture" or symbols of "cultural images" should be included in. He cannot tell what are the basic sources of his images and what are symbols forced in from outside. Multiple cultural symbols themselves are constituting a kind of symbol culture. Therefore, while artists experience, perceive and express this symbol culture consciously and sensitively, their own rational spirit and will to power often cause them to question this culture and make detailed inquiries about its foundation and reason of existence. Hu Zhiying is just an artist sensitive and good at questioning. Just because he is sensitive, multiple, numerous and jumbled visual images are represented in his art, making us seem to sense the aimlessness and richness of life in disorder and antagonism, as if things are shuttling and colliding in limitless time and space, and a stretch of enchanting red, like a vortex with tremendous energy, makes transient lives dizzy as ephemeras are. Consciousness flashes just as jumping. On the other hand, because he is good at questioning, we sense, in the aimlessness and dizziness through time and space, the existence of a kind of rational power which questions the existence and structure of a culture, as if questioning the significance and value of the existence of life. This questioning, especially in the out-of-order cultural situation, needs the power of will with which to question transiency.

Therefore, Hu Zhiying got himself into trouble with his brilliant paper *About the Transiency of Art*, and the mere presentation of his personal meditation was considered a challenge to the so-called authority. If will and character can conquer earthliness, the desire for personal fame and gain, and one's cowardice, they cannot confront the power and authority representing the "culture", for power has the right to refuse to debate with him face to face. According to Foucault, discourse and power are so linked that without power there would be no discourse and without discourse power would also be meaningless. It just confirms Hu Zhiying's viewpoint: if art and culture are transient, is power permanent?

The main problem of culture is that of power; in a broader context, "Western Culturalism" with the West as its center of power and "Orientalism" of the East in which one is forced to resist his will and to follow the sub-consciousness form a situation in which powers are re-allocated and they collide with each other, resist each other, and will dissolve. The subtext and potential possibilities of the discourse elements and tendencies of different cultures shown in this situation are always connected with the right of attendance and the right of presence. The advancing and accepting of the same cultural problem, for example, "Identity and Difference" (the theme of the *46th Venice Biennale*), are expressed by the East and the West with their respective power discourse, and in this process they both try to embody their power as much as possible. For regions, groups and individuals, the power of culture is also exposed and aggressive in its construction and existence. They all strive for the right to speak but their speeches interfere with and cancel out each other; they all strive for, and try to form, their own cultural power but they find that their own cultural power is so insignificant among multitudinous cultural powers of others that their powers dissolve each other and are often violated and trampled on by powers beyond culture. All this seems to involve deepest helplessness, and what is more helpless lies in the fact that the cultural fortresses constituted by personal mentalities are mutually independent, they conflict with each other, they are unable to communicate with each other and they are helpless. Artists can meditate and question these problems of cultural psychology about juxtaposing, colliding and dissolving only within the limit of possibilities of perceiving and expressing and the range permitted by the authority.

Therefore, it seems that we can sense, in Hu Zhiying's works, the peeling off and representing, layer after layer, and disassembling and regrouping, time and again, of his personal cultural images. While at the same time, these cultural images not only have personal significance, but also point to a wider area and cultural space, raising questions full of reason and will about significant cultural constructions.

We can see that the unique feeling about the classical Song Dynasty paintings, the wild folk art and the expressiveness of ink and wash paintings and the tension with reason contained in it constitute the foundation of Hu Zhiying's personal cultural images. It seems that we can find some indications of the sources of his images in his early works of various types and in his interest in calligraphy and abstract ink and wash painting. In his recent works, we often see symbols from landscape paintings of the Southern Song Dynasty, even those obviously from Ma Yuan's *Walking While Singing*, folk color composition of red, black, gold and silver, folk materials of lacquering, and loca abstract elements with strong expressiveness of brush and ink; hence perhaps we can classify them among eastern style cultural images. However, the problem is not so simple and clear. When we accept something and even hope to take it as the basis for our absorption and regrouping, the most difficult problem we meet is perhaps our suspicion about this basis, and we become hesitative and perplexed in our absorption and regrouping. Maybe it is a process of consciousness, and also a process of the emergence and development of culture. Hu Zhiying attaches importance to the process of consciousness and represents the state of culture through it. So in his paintings, consciousness is unfolded layer after layer and cultural images are displayed one after another; questioning, suspecting and colliding become the cultural consciousness itself. In his paintings, we seem to sense a kind of suspicion about and reverence for Cezanne, the father of modern art; the attention to the collapse of the sense of time and space and the deep affection for the mysterious realm; the nostalgic yearning for and the dissolving of the sense of religion; the surpassing of the mental space and its freezing; the passionate casting of life itself and the rational analysis of it…It is with this multiplicity of these cultural images that Hu Zhiying attempts to construct a new layer of their meanings. If Hu Zhiying as an artist attains his purpose of expression through the process of juxtaposition and collision of different cultures, then Hu Zhiying as a rational contemplator takes this process as a starting point and examines and questions further the problem of the cultural power, and his conclusion tends to be "transiency": we cannot get a clear idea about the potential significance and the energy of power orientation of Song Dynasty art in public life relationship of contemporary China, and the cultural relationship constituted between this orientation and energy and modern or post-modern art in contemporary society; we cannot face the juxtaposition of the idyllic spiritual yearning exemplified by "walking while singing" and the stimulation of desire with violence and terror latent in it in the common mental space; we cannot accept a kind of ink dark religious meditation amid the red fanaticism and secular emotion instigation… Here, personal cultural power and social and public cultural power both resist and conflict with each other and conspire with and dissolve each other. When we think we have acquired a kind of cultural power and a mode of discourse and make a personal speech, we find helplessly in the end that our own discourse is in fact the result of the hint from (or the violation by) the discourse of the others, and the so-called power of our own is often a small gear in the weapon of power of the others, rotating helplessly and passively. Maybe this is what Hu Zhiying doubts and attempts to question about the culture with power as its pivot, but the result of this questioning is helpless. Therefore, he can only give his series of works a series of helpless titles: "The First Day of the Fifth Lunar Month of the Jisi Year, June 9; The Eleventh Day of the Fifth Lunar Month of the Yimao Year, June 19; The Twenty-First Day of the Fifth Lunar Month of the Jichou Year, June 29", "The First Day of the Ninth Lunar Month of the Guimao Year, October 20; The Eleventh Day of the Ninth Lunar Month of the Guichou Year, October 30; The Twenty-First Day of the Guihai Year, November 9", "Guiyou, The First Year of the Reign of King Zhending of Zhou (468 B.C.)", etc. You can certainly doubt the intention and meaning in using these titles that seem to have nothing to do with the paintings themselves, and it is in this doubt that Hu Zhiying's intention and meaning lie.

After all, Hu Zhiying is an artist, and most of the work of an artist lies in concrete technical operations or even those of a craftsman. Without these operations and degrees of difficulty in techniques, any doubt and questioning would be fog-like fantasy. Although Hu Zhiying feels helpless towards the cultural power of the outside world, he is quite clear about the will to power his own art should have. In other words, he has a clear direction in establishing his own art language, and he chooses to use lacquering, a sophisticated technique, in expressing contemporary culture and his thinking about it, and lays stress on, and even is very particular about, the enjoyability of color, materials (including canvas, wood plate, Yangjiang paint, lacquer, gold and silver powder and foil, and vermilion), symbols, lines and masses, and tries to construct his fortress of art discourse with them.

Of course my reading of Hu Zhiying in this way may not be meaningful for others, and may similarly be the result of the violation of the cultural power for Hu Zhiying himself, and this is exactly the helplessness of contemporary culture. I give an account of a kind of artistic existence and phenomenon with my own cultural power, while Hu Zhiying and others are constructing their own respective cultural fortresses with their own will of culture. In a post-modern society seemingly open and with unprecedented information coverage, deconstruction becomes a fashion and an inevitable choice. However, deconstruction does not mean demolishing the walls of the fortresses; instead, people are abusing and strengthening their own cultural power respectively with which to violate and dissolve others' power. The mutual strengthening and dissolving, the converging and mutual canceling out of power is just an inevitable tendency in the contemporary world culture.

(Originally published in *Jiangsu Art Monthly*, No. 2, 1997, published by Jiangsu Fine Arts Publishing House)

志颖和他的画

吕品田

 志颖和我，少时因习画相识，并经常在文化馆举办的画展上彼此欣赏尚且十分青涩的作品。那时候，大家画的都是现在所谓的"文革题材"，但彼此间的交流从不谈"思想"或"观念"，而总是谈技术，谈构图、线条、色彩，或谈人物造型及动作处理之类的东西，对艺术有一种堪称绝对的虔诚与单纯。

 志颖天性沉静，不爱言语，和大家在一起，嘿嘿一笑是他最经常的表达方式。当时他多画工笔画，画作像他的性格一样文静。（图1）现在回想起来，他在事艺作风上有一种我们这些伙伴们所不具有的少年老成的沉稳。尽管传统在那个年代备受冲击，但志颖显然还是一一做过诗、书、画、印的功课。这惠益对他是深远的。他以后所追求的解构艺术作风，因此缘故而能从容地遣调"文化影像"。当然，其少时的童子功，意义并不局限于此。

 后来，我们上大学、谋生计，各奔东西，都离开了家乡，往来不像以前那么多那么直接了，但偶尔的联系却总是带起彼此从未了断的顾念。

 志颖定居于广州，在那里先后读了硕士、博士，如今执教于华南师范大学美术学院。他学养全面、视野开阔，于艺术的创作和研究都有精专的涉猎，成果丰硕，事业干得十分出色。不同于一般的画家，他主事绘画还潜心学术，勤于思考且善于思辨，是实践和理论兼重兼得的艺术家。多年来，他笔耕不辍、著述不断，发表出版了好些论文、专著或译著，论思涉及绘画、书法、文学、艺术教学和西方现代艺术等诸多方面，在艺术界颇有影响。

 志颖的绘画是独特而颖异的，在国内画坛堪称独树一帜。以我之见，其绘画上的种种独特性或新颖性，并不突兀，自有合乎其个人经历和情理的由来。

 中国传统艺术的童子功（图2）和刻骨铭心的文化眷恋，时代际遇和艺术探索为之打开的西方艺术视界，让他或许不像许多为风潮所动的前卫艺术家那样，深切地感受到一种影响其内心世界和艺术观的文化张力。构成这种张力的两个文化感受源，对他来说都是那般的博大雄厚。他无法在自己的内心深处调解所感受到的彼此的差异性冲突，似乎也难以把自己的灵魂单纯地寄托于任何一方。天性沉静、不爱言语的志颖，因而有了由思想认识所引发的精神张力——一种有如箭在弦上、张而未发般"紧张"的心理情结。这种心理因素酝酿着满腔的不断升腾的热情，孕育着终究需要释怀的强烈表现欲和缤纷形式感。"我无法抑制地需要某些特别的方式表达自己"——志颖深切地感觉到了已然蕴蓄的内在张力，他需要切合内省经验地尽情表达。呈现在我们眼前的、他的那些独特而颖异的画作，当是如其所愿的一种"既溶解理智的坚冰，又平息激情的喷薄；而以自然宿命和人为秩序统一内心深处无以名状的灵魂语言，获得既稳定永恒，又给幻想玄思以极大空间的表达方式"。

 画作所透露的心理图式，似乎让少时的志颖在我的视界里远去。而迎面过来的这一志颖，如其画上那一个一个的形式元素难以按常规来解读来连贯一样，也有着不能简单地加以揣摩的复杂内心世界。

 我不认为志颖是以故作玄奥的策略来制构惊世骇俗的所谓"现代性"，或者后现代所谓的"震惊"美学效果，因为那个曾经的闹市已经收场。志颖是敏感型的艺术家，他一定会敏锐地察觉时代的新的脉动。眼下现实中，最强劲的一种时代脉动，是"文化多样性"诉求在"全球化"情势中的逆势上扬。面对我未必揣摩得清楚的今天的志颖，我更愿意将他的艺术追求和价值实现置于这样一个时代场域和这样一种人文诉求来解读，以至于将他画上那些难以按常规来解读来连贯的形式元素，理解为突破单一文明价值观和单一文化认知图式的新世界的拼图。志颖的自述，或许可以支持我的这种难免主观的解读——对于自己的表达需要，他认为无法固定于某一种模式或风格而要诉诸相互冲突、迥然不同的状态或方式，并强调："只有两种或多种强烈反差的情绪和思维活动所形成的广阔巨大的空间方能满足我的这一需要。我一直以来都倾心于我以为十分重要的'文化反差'，因而我的作品常常出现东西方不同元素的交织，通过多种材料甚至综合媒介来表达这一反差，最终的效果却又皈依于单纯。"以我的直观感受，志颖的解构艺术作风和画面处理，在视觉地呈现文化的"反差"方面，的确非常有力。

 在为"反差"而洒落幅间的那许多图形影像的碎片中，我惟恍惟惚地觉得少时的志颖不时迎面而来。那些依稀可辨的古典山水画片段、带笔墨意味的局部扫描、乡土格调的色彩处理以及大漆砄砾之类的典型中国材料，似乎是文化记忆的一种缄默提示，让我断断续续地感到某种暧昧的亲切。每当这会，我总是试想：志颖在遣调它们的时候会是怎样的一种心情。我对他的"嘿嘿一笑"印象太深，实在无法超拔，以至于总是想着能在某个"碎片"上追寻到自己的历史经验。这无疑是徒然的。如今，一切作为历史经验的"熟悉"，已在画里化作"无以名状的灵魂语言"，缄默着任你追问任你揣度。

 这便是"解构"的魅力。

 志颖的画上，"文化多样性"呈现为解构的缤纷的"文化影像"，它折射着艺术主体不以某种文化认同为归宿的"自我的解构"。集合于画面的一切，仅仅是"文化影像"的形式重组而非"文化认同"的意义建构。因此，他的绘画艺术让我们持续地感受到一种张力凸显的紧张感，也让我们持续地直面着一种画家所倾心的"文化反差"。这种基于相互冲突、迥然不同状态或方式的绝对化的"紧张"和"反差"，也许就是画家所希望的"皈依于单纯"的最终效果。在交织不同元素的画面上，你不必徒劳追问和揣度最终的东西，"单纯"就是单纯，一切如你所见。要知道，表现"解构的自我"，结果只会是"涵义复杂而不确定"；而对于"自我的解构"的表现，任何的心理反应或阅读理解都是确当的终极解读。

在我看来，志颖以自己的"解构的重组"方式，表达了稳定、永恒的"紧张"与"反差"，他的画真是任人幻想玄思……

在幻想玄思中，我惟恍惟惚地见他嘿嘿一笑！

（原载《在幻象锁链的彼岸——胡志颖绘画作品1989–2009》，中国环球文化出版社，2010）

（图1）节临《八十七神仙卷》，1978，宣纸上水墨，23×43cm
(Fig. 1) A copy of party the *87 Immortals*, 1978, ink and wash on rice paper, 23 × 43 cm

Zhiying and His Paintings

By Lv Pintian

Zhiying and I got to know each other in our boyhood when we were both learning to paint and often went to enjoy each other's then immature works at the exhibitions held by the cultural center. In those days, we both created paintings about what is now called "the Cultural Revolution theme", but the discussions between us never dealt with "thoughts" or "conceptions"; instead, we always talked about skills, about lines, compositions, colors, or such topics as depiction of figures and treatment of movements, with an absolutely devout and pure attitude toward art.

Zhiying is a quiet man of few words by nature, and when staying with us, a slight laughter is his usual way to express himself. At that time, most of his paintings were done in a meticulous style (Fig. 1), gentle and quiet as his character. In retrospect, he possessed, in his manner of doing art, a precocious prudence we, as his companions, did not possess. Though traditional things suffered from attacks in those years, Zhiying evidently practised hard to master the basic skills of poetry, calligraphy, painting and seal cutting, and this benefited him profoundly. Therefore, when he pursued the style of deconstructive art later, he could maneuver "cultural images" at ease. Of course, the solid basis laid in his youth means much more than this.

Later, we both left our hometown and went to different places to attend college and then to make a living. Since then the contacts between us are not so frequent and direct as before, but occasional ones always arouse our mutual care ever lingering in our mind.

Zhiying has settled down in Guangzhou, where he has obtained a master's degree and a doctor's degree successively, and now he teaches at the College of Fine Arts, South China Normal University. With erudite knowledge and a wide vision, he has achieved great successes in both artistic creation and research. Unlike common painters, with painting as his main pursuit, he also devotes himself to academic research. Diligent in thinking and good at speculation, he is an artist who has done well in both theory and practice. Over the years, he has kept writing and published a number of treatises, monographs and translations. With their subjects ranging from painting, calligraphy, literature, teaching of art to modern Western art, they are quite influential in the art circles.

The paintings of Zhiying are distinctive and original, and can be said to constitute a unique school in the domestic painting circles. In my opinion, the distinctiveness and originality of his paintings, rather than ungrounded, is reasonable and conformable to his personal experience.

His solid grounding in traditional Chinese art (Fig. 2), his deep affection for culture, and his contact with Western art made possible by the opportunity of the times and his art research, make him, perhaps unlike many avant-garde artists susceptible to the trends, feel deeply a kind of cultural tension which has an influence on his inner world and view of art. Both of the two sources of cultural sensation constituting this tension are so rich and profound for him that he cannot mediate the conflict between their mutual differences he feels at the bottom of his heart, and it seems hard for him to find spiritual sustenance in either single side. Zhiying, a quiet man of few words by nature, thus has a spiritual tension resulting from his ideological understanding — a "tense" psychological complex like an arrow on the bowstring waiting to be shot. This psychological factor leads to the brewing of enthusiasm which keeps rising in his heart, a strong desire of expression to be released earlier or later, and a profuse sense of form. "I need uncontrollably some special modes to express myself." — Zhiying has deeply felt the already latent inner tension, and he has the need to express himself to his heart's content in a manner fit in with his introspective experience. His distinctive and original paintings before our eyes are exactly what he desires them to be: "both to melt the hard ice of reason and subside the outburst of passion; to unify the language of the soul beyond description in the depth of human mind with natural fatalism and man-made order and obtain a stable and eternal mode of expression that will provide enormous space for illusion and fantasy."

The psychological schema revealed in his paintings seems to make me feel that the young Zhiying is fading away in my field of vision, while the present Zhiying before us has a complicated inner world we cannot figure out in a simple way, just as the formal elements in his paintings cannot be read or made coherent in a conventional way.

I don't think that Zhiying is trying to create an astounding "modernity" or a so called "shocking" aesthetic effect of postmodernism by using the tactic of deliberately being abstruse, for the once boisterous scene is already over. As a sensitive artist, Zhiying must be able to perceive the new pulse of the times acutely. The most powerful pulse of the times at present is the rise of the appeal of "cultural diversity" against the general tendency of "globalization". As for the Zhiying of today whom perhaps I cannot figure out clearly, I prefer to read his pursuit of art and value realization in terms of such times context and such humanistic appeal that I understand the formal elements in his painting which one cannot understand or make coherent easily in a conventional way as a picture collage of a new world in which the unitary values of civilization and unitary schema of cultural cognition are broken. Perhaps his self-account can serve as a support of my unavoidably subjective reading. He thinks that, due to his won need of expression, he cannot limit himself to a certain mode or style, but should resort to conflicting and utterly different states or ways, and says emphatically, "Only the vast and enormous space formed by two or more kinds of sharply contrastive moods and thinking activities can satisfy this need of mine. I have been engrossed all along in the 'cultural contrast' which I think very important, and therefore interweavement of different elements of the East and the West often appears in my works. I try to express this contrast through various materials and even mixed media but the final effect remains simple." I feel intuitively that Zhiying's artistic style of deconstruction and treatment of his pictures are indeed effective in presenting the "cultural contrast" visually.

Among the fragments of images scattering in his paintings for the sake of expressing the "contrast", I feel that the young Zhiying seems to come up to me at times. The vaguely discernible fragments of classical landscape paintings, the partial scanning with brush stroke effects, the treatment of color with local style, and typical Chinese materials such as Chinese lacquer and vermilion, seem to be a silent hint of cultural memory, making me feel a surge of warm feeling from time to time. At such moments, I always wonder what mental state he was in when he maneuvered them. His "slight laughter" has impressed me so deeply that I always attempt to find my own historical experiences in one of such "fragments". This is no doubt in vain. Now, all the "familiarity", as historical experience, has been reduced to "an indescribable language of the soul" in his paintings keeping silent for you to inquire into or conjecture about.

This is the charm of "deconstruction".

The embodiment of "cultural diversity" in the form of a profusion of deconstructive "cultural images" in the paintings by Zhiying reflects the "self-deconstruction" of the artist not

〔图2〕黄山图，1985，宣纸上水墨，68×134cm
(Fig. 2) *Huangshan Mountains*, 1985, ink and wash on rice paper, 68 × 134 cm

taking a certain cultural identity as his destination. All things included in his painting are merely a formal regrouping of "cultural images" rather than a meaning construction of "cultural identity". Therefore, in his paintings we feel continuously an obvious tension, and face continuously the "cultural contrast" the artist has made great efforts to express. This absolutised "tension" and "contrast" based upon conflicting and utterly different states or modes may be the final effect of "remaining simple" the painter hopes to achieve. In the paintings in which different elements are interwoven together, you need not make a futile effort to inquire into or conjecture about something final. "Simple" is simple, and everything is as you see it. You should know that, the expression of "deconstructed self" can only result in the "complexity and uncertainty of meaning"; while any psychological reaction to or understanding of the expression of "self-deconstruction" is proper ultimate reading.

In my opinion, Zhiying expresses the stable and perpetual "tension" and "contrast" in his own manner of "deconstructive regrouping". His painting really allows any fantasy and meditation…

In fantasy and meditation, I seem to see his slight laughter!

(Originally published in the *Beyond the Chains of Illusion — Hu Zhiying's Paintings 1989-2009*, China Global Culture Publishing House, 2010)

一个人的海市蜃楼

——关于胡志颖和他的艺术

杨 卫

在中国当代艺术界，胡志颖是一位非常特殊的人物。这种特殊性不仅在于他的特立独行，从来不与潮流为伍，更在于他的学术身份，即作为一个画家，却赢取过文艺学博士的桂冠。正是因为这样的理论嗜好，与艺术的直觉相联系，使胡志颖超越了一般画家的感受，而又没有职业理论家的那种酸腐之气。我认为，要研究胡志颖的艺术，必须得结合他的文艺思想，只有将他的理论思考与艺术实践看作一个有机的整体，我们才能进入胡志颖的艺术世界，找到一把理解他探索实践的钥匙。

早在2002年，胡志颖就获得了暨南大学的文艺学博士学位，而他的博士论文完全与绘画无关，涉及的是文学，侧重于语言分析。他的博士论文为《文学彼岸性研究》。（图1）这是一个关于语言哲学的命题，以文学的彼岸性，即语言的极限思维作为研究对象，其抵达的幽暗层次与文化深度，很容易让人窒息，以至于变得束手无策，甚至虚无缥缈。而胡志颖却能够沉浸于这种晦暗幽闭的窒息之中，精研锐思，条分缕析，从中找到一条思想的出路，足可以反映他的思辨能力与理论素质。很难想象一个热衷于形象思维的画家，会对如此艰深的理论发生兴趣，如果不是心灵受到过彼岸世界的召示，人很难有这样的思想诉求。我总想，胡志颖在绘画创作上保持自己的独立姿态，不为潮流所动，其内在的原因可能就在于此，在于他一以贯之的终极关怀。

当然，胡志颖并非不食人间烟火，更不是逃避现实。恰恰相反，他对终极问题的热衷，根本上还是为了给我们存在的这个时空注入一种人文深度。这就像他在文学的彼岸性研究中旁征博引一样，他的绘画创作也无不关乎着当代人的生命体验，与时代精神紧密相联。纵观胡志颖从事绘画创作的历史，我们能够看到他的个人线索与各个时期的文化思潮之间的共振关系。比如1979年他就创作过有关"红卫兵"伤害题材的作品，（图2）这与当年的"伤痕美术"思潮几乎是处在同一个起跑线；再比如他在1989年前后创作的一批"抽象水墨"，以一些东方的神秘符号为元素，也无不表现了在西方现代艺术的影响下寻找主体意识的突围。实际上，这跟"85新潮"以来，中国现代艺术整体呈现出的影响焦虑，也有着藕断丝连的内在联系……看得出来，胡志颖在绘画创作上并不是闭门造车，而是一直带着当代人的问题意识往前推进，只不过受终极理想的价值启迪，他没有浅尝辄止，把自己探索的步伐停止于某个思潮或某个现实问题而已。

正是因为胡志颖的这种不懈探索精神，驱使他一次次地超越自我，将自己的绘画艺术不断引向历史的纵深，到后来与更大的文化背景联系在了一起。二十世纪九十年代以后，胡志颖在从事了一段时间"抽象水墨"的试验之后，画画逐渐隐现出了一些传统山水画的意象。这可以理解为胡志颖对现实世界的超越，已经不再是简单地关心现实问题，而是遨游于浩瀚汪洋的历史大海，将自我的现实纳入到了文化传统的悠悠长河之中。我注意过胡志颖对中国传统山水画的意象捕捉，并不是元明成熟起来的文人山水，而是倾向于早期的北宋山水画，即还没有形成笔墨传统之前那种直面山川的表达。事实上，山水画自从被文人截取，形成"寄乐于画"（董其昌）的传统之后，山水的意向便已经与文人的情怀融合在一起，原本的敬畏之心就逐渐被"墨戏"所取代了。但在笔墨还没有突显之前，比如北宋时期的山水画，那里面透露出来的生疏感，以及突兀与奇异的效果，还折射着人们面对自然时的某种恐惧。我由此想到胡志颖为什么没有选择元明的文人山水，而是独独钟爱于北宋之前的山水画？原因就在于他对彼岸世界的眷念，已经使他感受了太多的精神历险。

事实上，险象环生的境遇，早就构成了胡志颖艺术作品的一个核心内容。这就像他涉及到中国传统山水画意象的系列绘画，作品的表征往往还布满了繁杂的生命图腾一样。如此这般剪不断理还乱的表现方式，体现了胡志颖对现实社会错综复杂的感受。而就这种现实感受来说，在他2007年前后创作的一批组画中表现得最为强烈。我们从中看到了胡志颖对现实世界的挣扎与反抗。也许正是因为感受到了现实社会的诸多困境，胡志颖才憧憬于彼岸，在他的文艺理论与艺术创作中不断寻找超越的契机。这也正所谓"愤怒出诗人"，重要的是有愤怒，还有良知。只是对于胡志颖而言，这种愤怒和良知，已经被他深厚的理论修养转换成了某种文化理想，以及不断超越自我的人文精神。

（原载《在幻象锁链的彼岸——胡志颖绘画作品1989-2009》，中国环球文化出版社，2010）

（图1）胡志颖著作《文学彼岸性研究》
(Fig. 1) Hu Zhiying's work *On the Palamitality in Literature*

（图2）无辜，1979，纸上水粉，80×120cm
(Fig. 2) *Innocent*, 1979, gouache on paper, 80 × 120 cm

The Mirage of a Single Person

— About Hu Zhiying and His Art

By Yang Wei

In the world of contemporary Chinese art, Hu Zhiying is a very particular person. This particularity consists not only in his being independently minded and keeping from the tide, but also in his academic identity, that is, though a painter, he has obtained a doctor's degree in the study of art and literature. It is the combination of predilection for theory and artistic intuition that enables Hu to excel common painters in sensibility and to be free from the pedantry of professional theorists. In my opinion, to make a study of Hu's art, we must take into account his thought on art and literature, and only if we view his theoretical reflections and artistic practice as an organic whole will we be able to enter the art world of Hu and to find the key to the understanding of his exploration and practice.

As early as 2002, Hu obtained a doctor's degree in the study of art and literature at Jinan University. His doctoral thesis has nothing to do with painting, but deals with literature instead, with emphasis on linguistic analysis. His thesis is titled *On the Paramitality in Literature*. (Fig. 1) As a proposition of linguistic philosophy, it takes the Paramitality in literature, i.e. the ultimate lingual thinking as its object of research and reaches such a degree of obscurity from cultural depth that one will feel suffocated, helpless, or even illusory. It suffices to show Hu's speculative ability and theoretical level that he can find a way out, in terms of thinking, in such an obscure and suffocating state by researching in depth and making analysis carefully and in detail. It is hard to imagine that a painter, who is keen on thinking in images, will take an interest in such an abstruse theory. Without being summoned by the world of the Paramita, one could hardly have such an ideological pursuit. I always think that the internal reason why Hu maintains his independence in his artistic creation, insusceptible to the tide, probably lies in this, in his consistent ultimate concern.

Certainly, Hu is not indifferent about mundane affairs and does not shun reality. On the contrary, fundamentally speaking, it is for the sake of adding a humanistic depth to the time and space we live in that he is keen on ultimate problems. Just as he quotes copiously from many sources in his thesis "On the Paramitality in Literature", all of his painting creations have something to do with life experience of contemporaries, and is closely connected to the spirit of the age. Taking a sweeping view of the history of his painting creation, we can see a resonant relationship between his paintings and cultural trends of thought of various periods. For example, the painting about the trauma of the "Red Guards" he produced in 1979 (Fig. 2) is almost on the same starting line with the "Trauma Art" trend of thought of that time. For another example, all the "abstract ink and wash paintings" with some Eastern mystic symbols as elements he produced around 1989 manifest, without exception, his attempt to find a breakthrough of subjective consciousness under the influence of modern Western art. Actually, this has some inner relation with the anxiety of influence that the whole modern Chinese art showed after the "'85 New Trend".... Obviously, Hu does not engage in painting creation irrespective of external circumstances; instead, he proceeds with the problem consciousness of a contemporary, only that inspired by the value of ultimate ideal, he is not satisfied with a superficial attempt and has not confined himself to a certain trend of thought or practical problem.

It is this spirit of persevering exploration that makes him surpass himself again and again and bring his art of painting to the depth of history continuously so that it is connected with the larger cultural background afterwards. After he made some experiments on "abstract ink and wash" for a period in the 1990s, there emerged some images from traditional landscape paintings in his works. It can be understood in this way: his transcendence of the real world no longer lies in merely concerning himself with practical problems; instead, he now swims in the boundless sea of history, bringing his own personal reality into the long river of cultural tradition. I have noticed that the images from landscape paintings Hu captured is not those from the matured literati landscape paintings of the Yuan and Ming Dynasties but those from the early landscape paintings of the Northern Song Dynasty, that is, the direct depictions of mountains and rivers before the brush and ink tradition came into being. In fact, since the scholars took over the art of landscape painting and the tradition of "painting for pleasure" (Dong Qichang) formed, images of landscape painting have been blended with thoughts and feelings of scholars, and the original awe has been replaced by the "ink play" gradually. However, the unskilledness and the abrupt and fantastic effect manifested in the landscape paintings done before brush and ink gained dominance, for example in those of the Northern Song Dynasty, still reflect man's fear before nature. This brings me the question: why has Hu not chosen the literati landscape paintings of the Yuan and Ming Dynasties but is interested solely in those of the Northern Song Dynasty in stead? The reason is that his deep affection for the world of Paramita has led him to too many spiritual adventures.

In fact, the experience of being beset by dangers has long become a core content of his art works. For instance, his series of paintings involving images from traditional Chinese landscape paintings are often fraught with miscellaneous totems of life. Such anfractuous representations reflect his complicated feeling of the real world. This practical feeling is manifested most strongly in a group of series he produced around 2007. We have seen in them his struggle and resistance against the real world. Perhaps just because he has experienced so many predicaments of the real world, Hu longs for the world of the Paramita, and keeps looking for chances to surpass the real world in his literary theory and artistic creation. Just as the saying goes, "anger produces a poet". In fact, the important thing is the presence of anger and conscience. Only as far as Hu Zhiying is concerned, due to his profound mastery of theories, this anger and conscience have been transformed into a certain cultural ideal and the humanistic spirit of continuous self transcendence.

(Originally published in the *Beyond the Chains of Illusion — Hu Zhiying's Paintings 1989-2009*, China Global Culture Publishing House, 2010)

胡志颖的艺术与中国当下风格化、样式化的艺术不同。他对东西方艺术的领悟都非常深，因此他自如驾驭东西绘画技巧表达特有的纵横古今的思维和情绪，让我们感受到特殊的心理欲求与体验，其绘画呈现的视觉感受新异而刺激，富于张力，先打眼，后撞心，动人心旌。

看胡志颖的绘画，你可以感觉到他的思路、他的理念、他所表现的风格非常独特、非常自我。他的心理世界可能不是一般人所能进入和理解的。这使得他的艺术很另类、很特殊。他是一个特别变化型的人，你很难把握他，他不是那种恒定不变的艺术家。他的思维是很艺术的，气质也是很艺术的。

胡志颖是一位特立独行并富于思想的当代艺术家。

——梅墨生

Hu Zhiying's art is different from the stylized and patternized art in present China. His profound comprehension of both Eastern and Western art enables Hu Zhiying to operate with Eastern and Western techniques of painting with ease in expressing specific ideas and feelings relating to ancient and modern times. In his works we can sense a special psychological desire and experience. His paintings are novel, stimulating and full of tension. They first catch the eye and then touch the heart of the viewer.

Beholding Hu Zhiying's paintings, you may feel that his train of thought, his ideas and his style are all very distinctive and individualized. His psychological world may be not accessible or comprehensible by ordinary people. This makes his art alternative and special. He is a man in such constant change that you cannot comprehend him easily. He is not an artist adhering to a constant type. He is artistic both in thinking and in temperament.

Hu Zhiying is an independently minded and thoughtful contemporary artist.

— Mei Mosheng

日历，1992-1995-2004，布上综合媒介，200×180cm
Calendar, 1992-1995-2004, mixed media on canvas, 200 × 180 cm

重造培根——狒狒与修女，2005，布上油彩、丙烯、大漆，196×153cm
Remake Bacon — Baboon and Nun, 2005, oil, acrylic and lacquer on canvas, 196 × 153 cm

重造培根——狒狒与修女（局部）
Remake Bacon — Baboon and Nun (detail)

重造培根——蝙蝠与玫瑰（1），2004–2005，布上油彩、丙烯、大漆，196×153cm
Remake Bacon — Bat and Rose (1), 2004-2005, oil, acrylic and lacquer on canvas, 196 × 153 cm

重造培根——蝙蝠与玫瑰（2），2004–2005，布上油彩、丙烯、大漆，196×153cm
Remake Bacon — Bat and Rose (2), 2004-2005, oil, acrylic and lacquer on canvas, 196 × 153 cm

重造培根——蝙蝠与玫瑰（3），2004–2005，布上油彩、丙烯、大漆，196×153cm
Remake Bacon — Bat and Rose (3), 2004-2005, oil, acrylic and lacquer on canvas, 196 × 153 cm

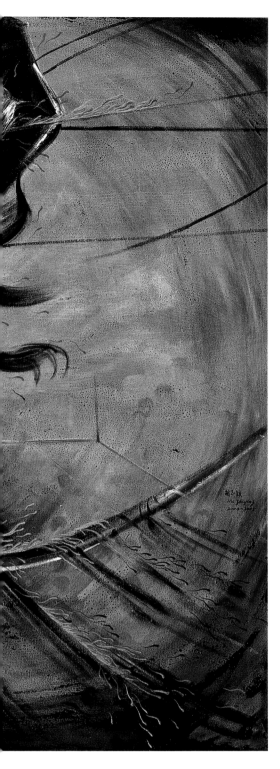

2000年后的绘画《重造培根》系列作品，在原有的基础上借鉴培根的艺术的元素更突出强烈造型的力量，更为直接进入人的灵魂对白或独白。通过油彩、丙烯与中国特有的材料大漆在不同层次上的交替使用，让作品产生一种超常的特殊效果，而这是与借用培根艺术元素汇合以别种元素所造就的幽冥气氛相表里的。激越的笔触和强烈的色彩反差表现那非常规的奇谲造型和灵魂世界，绘画性和深邃意境并驾齐驱，涵义复杂而不确定。

——胡志颖

On the original basis, *Remake Bacon*, a series after 2000, draws on elements of Bacon's art, and gives prominence to the power of depiction, entering into spiritual dialogues or monologues of human beings more directly. In this series, an extraordinary and special effect is achieved through alternate use of oils, acrylic and Chinese lacquer, a material peculiar to China, at different layers. This is interlinked with the gloomy atmosphere caused by combination of borrowed elements of Bacon's art with other elements. The unconventional and grotesque shapes and spiritual world are portrayed in vehement brush strokes and strong contrast of colors. Painterliness is on a par with profound artistic conception, and the implication is complex and uncertain.

— Hu Zhiying

人的精神本体与客观的实存本体相互作用的无限多样，关联着精神本体对实存本体认知的不可穷尽。
——胡志颖

The infinite diversity of the forms of the interaction between spiritual noumenon and existential noumenon of the human beings entails the inexhaustibility of the cognition of the existential subject by the spiritual subject.
— Hu Zhiying

重造培根——蝙蝠与玫瑰（1）（局部）
Remake Bacon — Bat and Rose (1) (detail)

重造培根──女子角斗（1），2004–2005，布上油彩、丙烯、大漆，196×153cm
Remake Bacon — Female Wrestling (1), 2004-2005, oil, acrylic and lacquer on canvas, 196 × 153 cm

重造培根──女子角斗（2），2004–2005，布上油彩、丙烯、大漆，196×153cm
Remake Bacon — Female Wrestling (2), 2004-2005, oil, acrylic and lacquer on canvas, 196 × 153 cm

重造培根──女子角斗（3），2004–2005，布上油彩、丙烯、大漆，196×153cm
Remake Bacon — Female Wrestling (3), 2004-2005, oil, acrylic and lacquer on canvas, 196 × 153 cm

因为胡志颖对两幅画中的形象都进行了比培根通常所做的更大的意象性解构，结果形成了这样一种构图，甚至尽管保留了培根的整体的构图冲击力和基调，实际上却似乎引用了朱利安·施纳贝尔（Julian Schnabel）的抽象性的某些方面。……胡志颖对多元文化的潮流作出重要的说明，在这股潮流中，将往昔、现今和未来的画家们联系在一起的影响、灵感与创新相交融。

——麦科马克

For Hu Zhiying has subjected the figures in both canvases to considerably more imagistic deconstruction than Bacon usually did, creating a composition that, in fact, appears to reference certain aspects of Julian Schnabel's abstractions even while retaining the overall compositional thrust and mood of Bacon…Hu Zhiying makes a major statement about the multicultural currents of cross-fertilization of influence, inspiration and innovation that unite painters of the past, present, and future.

— Ed McCormack

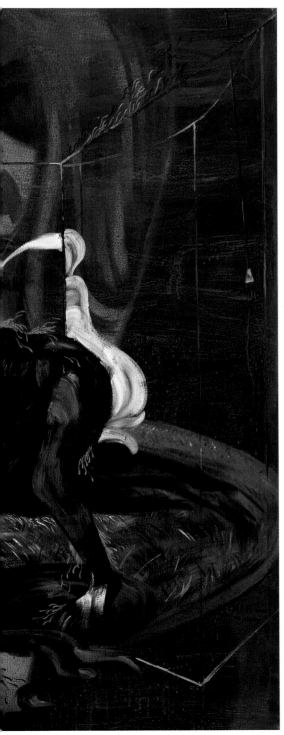

重造培根——女子角斗（2）（局部）
Remake Bacon — Female Wrestling (2) (detail)

重造培根——女子角斗（3）（局部）
Remake Bacon — Female Wrestling (3) (detail)

重造培根——山君与艳星（1），2005，布上油彩、大漆，196×153cm
Remake Bacon — Tige and Star (1), 2005, oil and lacquer on canvas, 196 × 153 cm

重造培根——山君与艳星（2），2005，布上油彩、大漆，196×153cm
Remake Bacon — Tige and Star (2), 2005, oil and lacquer on canvas, 196 × 153 cm

重造培根——山君与艳星（3），2005，布上油彩、大漆，196×153cm
Remake Bacon — Tige and Star (3), 2005, oil and lacquer on canvas, 196 × 153 cm

重造培根——山君与艳星（2）（局部）
Remake Bacon — Tige and Star (2) (detail)

重造培根——猫头鹰与灵长类（1），2006，布上油彩、丙烯、大漆，196×153cm
Remake Bacon — Owl and Primate (1) , 2006, oil, acrylic and lacquer on canvas, 196 × 153 cm

重造培根——猫头鹰与灵长类（2），2006，布上油彩、丙烯、大漆，196×153cm
Remake Bacon — Owl and Primate (2) , 2006, oil, acrylic and lacquer on canvas, 196 × 153 cm

重造培根——猫头鹰与灵长类（3），2006，布上油彩、丙烯、大漆，196×153cm
Remake Bacon — Owl and Primate (3) , 2006, oil, acrylic and lacquer on canvas, 196 × 153 cm

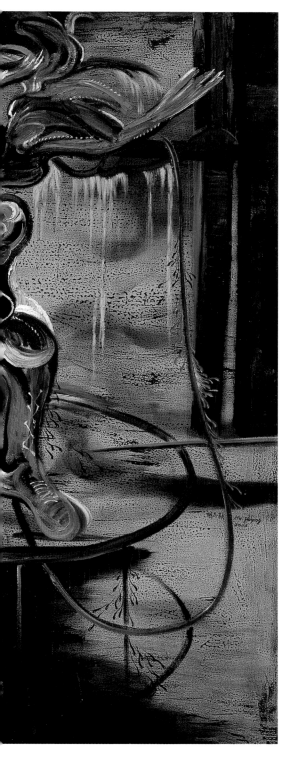

胡志颖命题奇异，思路幽玄，很有一些特立独行的游侠色彩。

——赵一凡

Hu Zhiying, with his unusual propositions and profound and abstruse trains of thought, is something of an independently minded roving brave.

— Zhao Yifan

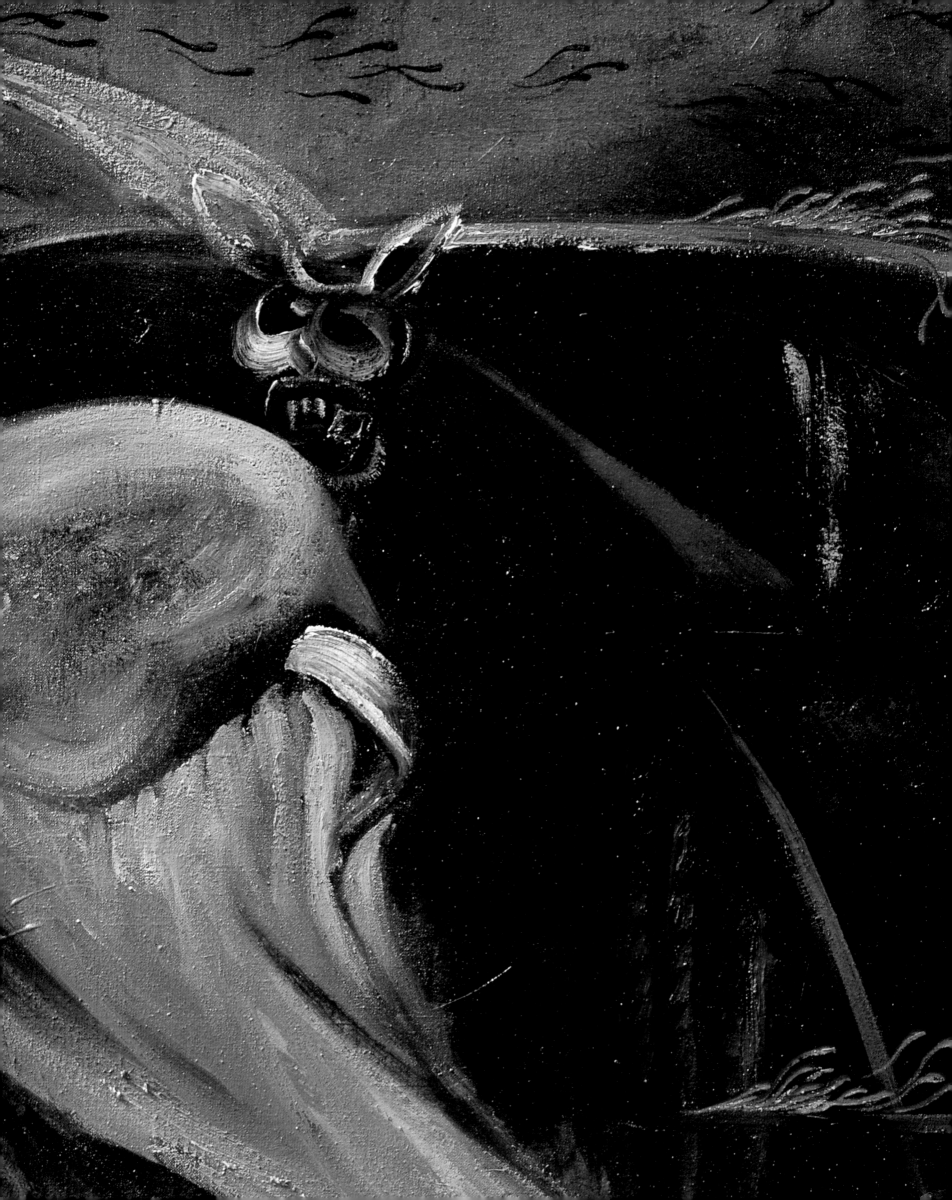

重造培根——猫头鹰与灵长类（1）（局部）
Remake Bacon — Owl and Primate (1) (detail)

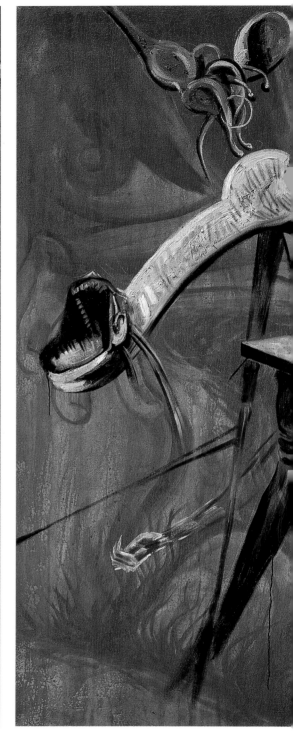

培根梦与性爱（1），2007，布上油彩、丙烯、大漆，192×153cm
Bacon's Dream and Sex (1), 2007, oil, acrylic and lacquer on canvas, 192 × 153 cm

培根梦与性爱（2），2007，布上油彩、丙烯、大漆，192×153cm
Bacon's Dream and Sex (2), 2007, oil, acrylic and lacquer on canvas, 192 × 153 cm

培根梦与性爱（3），2007，布上油彩、丙烯、大漆，192×153cm
Bacon's Dream and Sex (3), 2007, oil, acrylic and lacquer on canvas, 192 × 153 cm

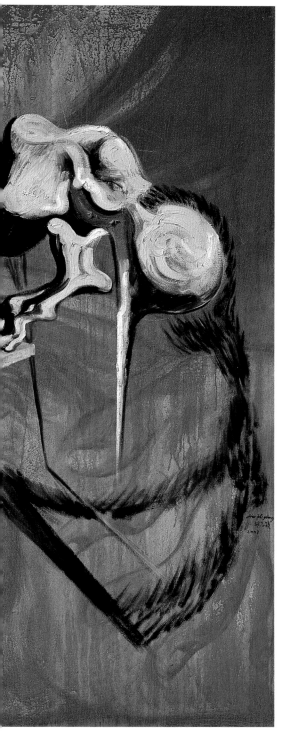

从胡志颖1989年的早期纸上水墨作品到他最近的向培根表示敬意的作品，他一直不墨守陈规，而是不断尝试将西方与东方影响的精髓融合起来。他从未有过机械的做法，联想有时是微妙的或者是明显的，但总是充满想象力。

——迪迪埃·赫希

From Hu Zhiying's early inks on paper in 1989 to his recent homage to Bacon, he has always travelled off the beaten path, but in a continuous attempt to combine the essence of western and eastern influences. He never had a mechanistic approach, and the associations can be subtle or obvious, but always imaginative.

— Didier Hirsch

培根梦与性爱（3）（局部）
Bacon's Dream and Sex (3) (detail)

169

性爱与文明之一，2008，布上油彩、丙烯、大漆，186×178cm
Sex and Civilization I, 2008, oil, acrylic and lacquer on canvas, 186 × 178 cm

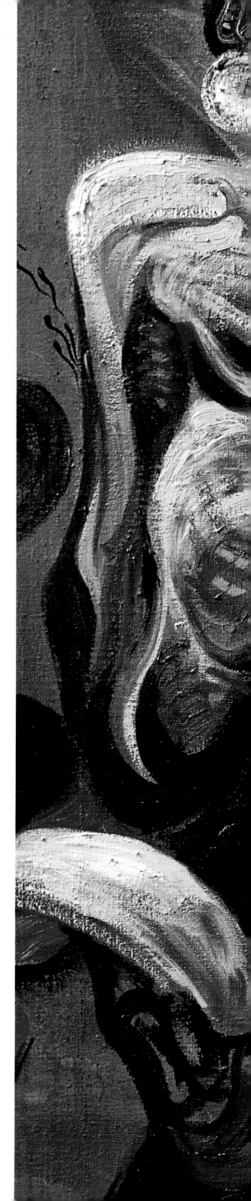

性爱与文明之一【局部】
Sex and Civilization I (detail)

在90年代，胡志颖在中国画坛上，以古典山水符号与西方视觉图像交织，形成特有的风格，呈现了一种与自然世界异乎寻常的关系，是东西方艺术的奇特沟通，天然成趣，与众不同。近年来，其作品则游弋于美与丑、生与死、此岸世界与彼岸世界之间，有时令人有种惊悚感。我被他作品强烈的视觉冲击力与震撼力所打动。

——李正天

In the painting circles of China in the 1990s, Hu Zhiying developed a distinctive style characterized by the interweaving of Chinese classic signs of mountains and waters with Western visual images. Presenting an extraordinary relationship with the natural world, this style, full of natural charm, embodied an unusual combination of Eastern art and Western art. In recent years, his works have wandered between beauty and ugliness, between life and death, and between this world and Faramita, sometimes making the beholder alarmed and frightened. I am touched by the strong visual impact and artistic charm of his works.

— Li Zhengtian

性爱与文明之二，2008，布上油彩、丙烯、大漆，186×178cm
Sex and Civilization II, 2008, oil, acrylic and lacquer on canvas, 186 × 178 cm

性爱与文明之三，2008，布上油彩、丙烯、大漆，196×153cm
Sex and Civilization III, 2008, oil, acrylic and lacquer on canvas, 196 × 153 cm

性爱与文明之四，2008，布上油彩、丙烯、大漆，196×153cm
Sex and Civilization IV, 2008, oil, acrylic and lacquer on canvas, 196 × 153 cm

性爱与文明之五，2008，布上油彩、丙烯、大漆，196×153cm
Sex and Civilization V, 2008, oil, acrylic and lacquer on canvas, 196 × 153 cm

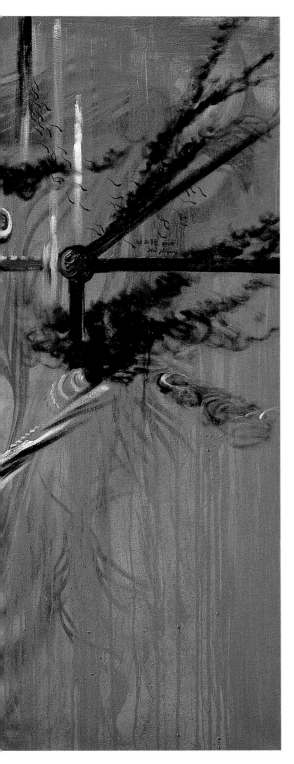

胡志颖与当下流行的风尚不一样。这位艺术家是就自己所关心的某种问题，长期用一种个人化的方式创作作品。他的作品可能关注的是更深层次的一些文化哲学问题。

——吴 鸿

Hu Zhiying does not follow the currently prevailing practice. He has produced works for a long time in an individualized way with an eye to certain problems he concerns himself with. He may have paid close attention in his works to some cultural and philosophical problems at a deeper level.

— Wu Hong

176　性爱与文明之五（局部）
Sex and Civilization V (detail)

性爱与文明之三（局部）
Sex and Civilization III (detail)

性爱与文明之四（局部）
Sex and Civilization IV (detail)

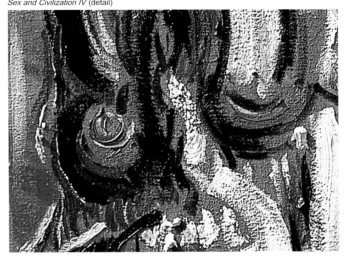

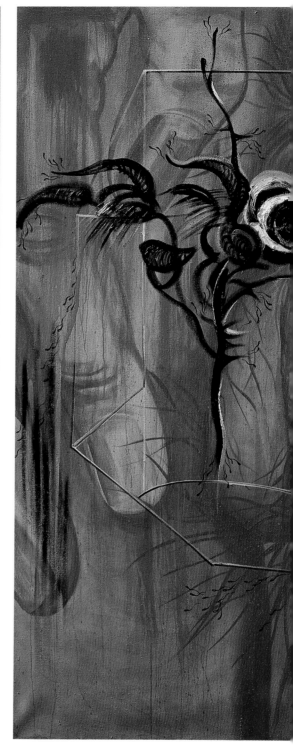

玫瑰之名之一，2009，布上油彩、丙烯、大漆，196×153cm
The Name of the Rose I, 2009, oil, acrylic and lacquer on canvas, 196 × 153 cm

玫瑰之名之二，2009，布上油彩、丙烯、大漆，196×153cm
The Name of the Rose II, 2009, oil, acrylic and lacquer on canvas, 196 × 153 cm

玫瑰之名之三，2009，布上油彩、丙烯、大漆，196×153cm
The Name of the Rose III, 2009, oil, acrylic and lacquer on canvas, 196 × 153 cm

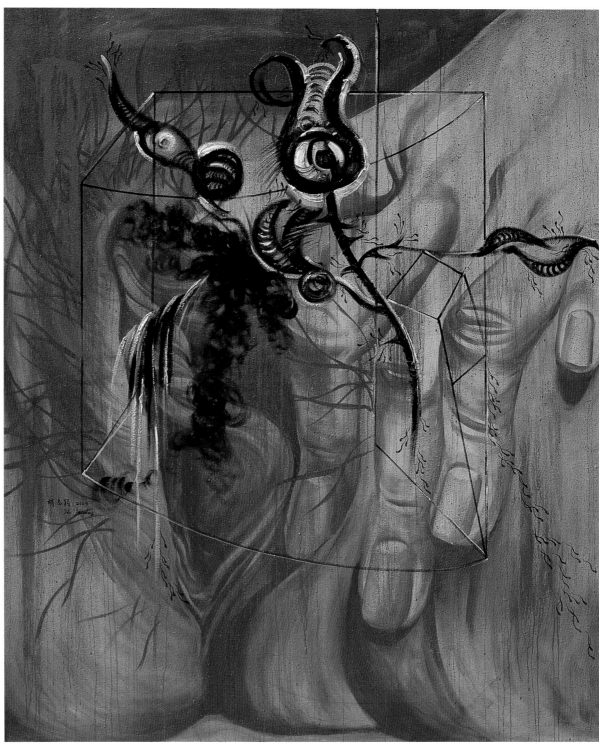

胡志颖个人按自己的需要，只按他自己某个阶段的内心需要，不管不顾，去做他的作品。从这个意义上，这倒符合艺术家的天性，也符合艺术的需要。

——贾方舟

Hu Zhiying has produced his works according to his personal need, or rather, according only to his internal need in a certain stage, regardless of other things. In this sense, this accords with the natural instinct of an artist, and also with the requirement of art.

— Jia Fangzhou

玫瑰之名之二（局部）
The Name of the Rose II (detail)

无常的态度，即是一种共生共存的态度，一种宽容的态度，它致使人们都将学会有自知之明；学会了解自己的动机、自己的生存方式以及他们各自的价值准则；同时也学会去发现，在这些特殊表现形式之外，他们还可以而且也应该分享着众多的美好希望和理想，反过来，这点又促使他们更加深入地了解在他们自己的文化中能够发现的带有普遍性的含义。无常观念的实质就是承认差别并尊重差别——这是尊重属于不同文化背景的人以及同一文化背景中不同人的尊严的基本方式。

——胡志颖

The attitude of transiency is an attitude of coexistence and tolerance. It makes people learn to know their own limitations, to know their own motives, their own ways of survival and their respective value standards, and at the same time to find that, besides these special manifestations, they can and should share numerous beautiful hopes and ideals. This will in turn further their understanding of the universal implications they can find in their own culture. The idea of transiency is in essence to acknowledge and respect differences. This is the basic way to respect the dignity of people of different cultural backgrounds or different people of the same cultural background.

— Hu Zhiying

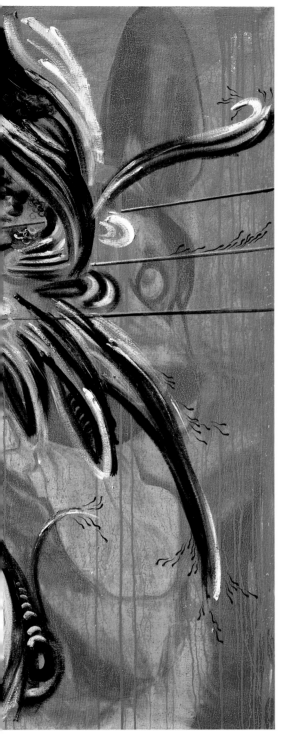

伸出你的舌头空荡荡（1），2009–2010，布上油漆、丙烯、大漆，196 × 153cm
Out Your Empty Tongue (1), 2009-2010, oil, acrylic and lacquer on canvas, 196 × 153 cm

伸出你的舌头空荡荡（2），2009–2010，布上油漆、丙烯、大漆，196 × 153cm
Out Your Empty Tongue (2), 2009-2010, oil, acrylic and lacquer on canvas, 196 × 153 cm

伸出你的舌头空荡荡（3），2009–2010，布上油漆、丙烯、大漆，196 × 153cm
Out Your Empty Tongue (3), 2009-2010, oil, acrylic and lacquer on canvas, 196 × 153 cm

伸出你的舌头空荡荡（1）（局部）
Out Your Empty Tongue (1) (detail)

胡志颖 2009
Hu Zhiying

伸出你的舌头空荡荡（2）（局部）
Out Your Empty Tongue (2) (detail)

伸出你的舌头空荡荡（3）（局部）
Out Your Empty Tongue (3) (detail)

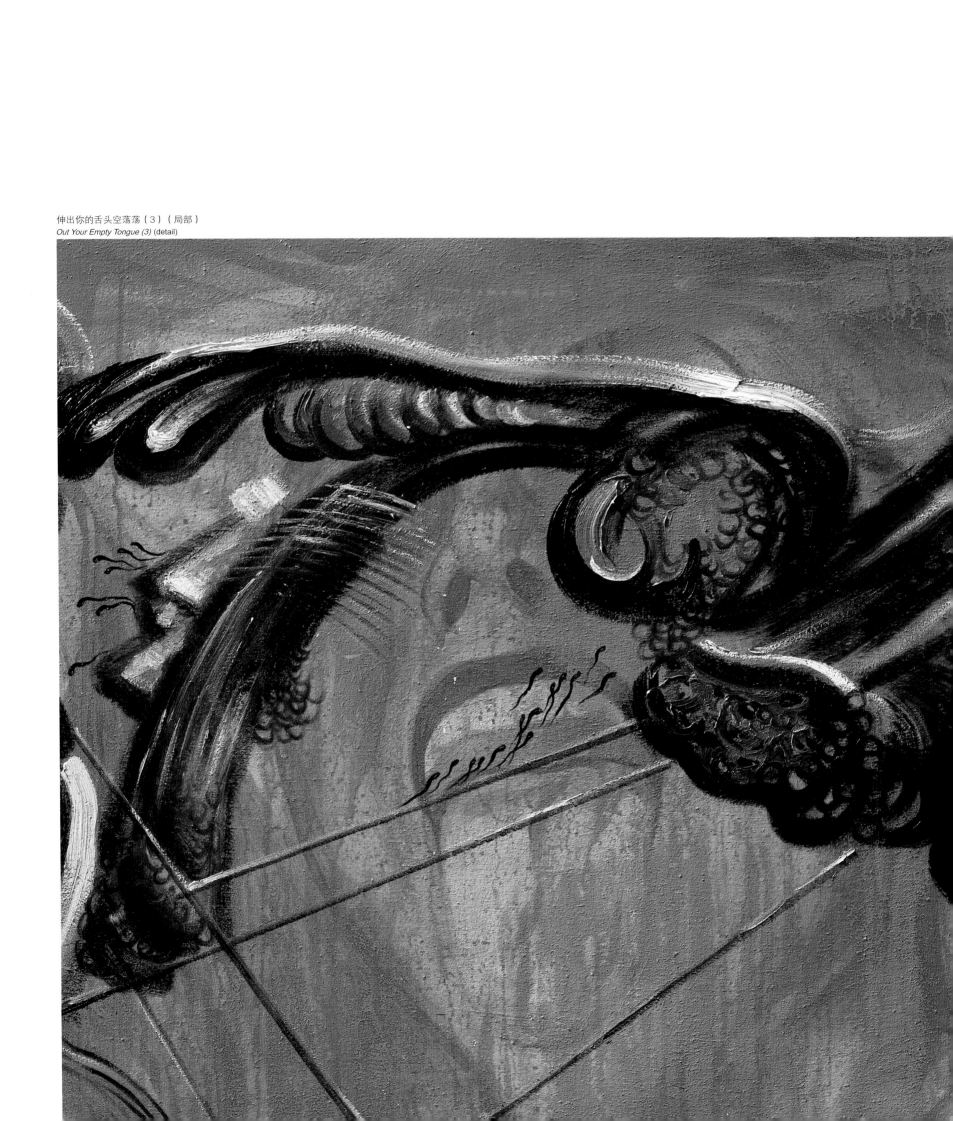

三位一体——仙花，神女，圣徒（1），2010，布上油彩、丙烯、大漆，206×163cm
Trinity — Fairy Flower, Goddess and Saint (1), 2010, oil, acrylic and lacquer on canvas, 206 × 163 cm

三位一体——仙花，神女，圣徒（2），2010，布上油彩、丙烯、大漆，206×163cm
Trinity — Fairy Flower, Goddess and Saint (2), 2010, oil, acrylic and lacquer on canvas, 206 × 163 cm

三位一体——仙花，神女，圣徒（3），2010，布上油彩、丙烯、大漆，206×163cm
Trinity — Fairy Flower, Goddess and Saint (3), 2010, oil, acrylic and lacquer on canvas, 206 × 163 cm

胡志颖是一位以文化哲学思考及体验为创作动力的艺术家。他既不关注社会现实的表层变化，也不关心个体心理及经验的表达，在二十多年的创作中，他唯一强调的是对终极命题的探寻，以及对某种可能的超然精神的无限接近。在这样的驱动力下，他的创作在各个阶段调节了水墨、大漆、油彩等各种媒介特性，也调动了不同文化中的诸多符号、形象与象征，通过对不同文化系统中的表征片段的错置与再造，暗示着文化的无常属性与幻象本质，并在这表征的裂缝中闪现着对存在的诗性直观。

——鲍　栋

Hu Zhiying is an artist with cultural philosophical meditation and experience as his motivation for creation. Caring about neither the superficial changes of social reality nor the expression of individual psychology and experience, he only stresses, during the 20 years of artistic creation, the search for the ultimate proposition and the infinite approach to some possible detached spirit. Under such a driving force, he has adjusted the characteristics of various mediums like ink and wash, lacquer, oil and others in his different phases of creation, and has also adopted many signs, images and symbols from various cultures. The dislocation and re-creation of representation fragments in different culture systems implies the transient nature and illusory essence of culture, and his poetic intuition of existence flashes in the cracks of these representations.

— Bao Dong

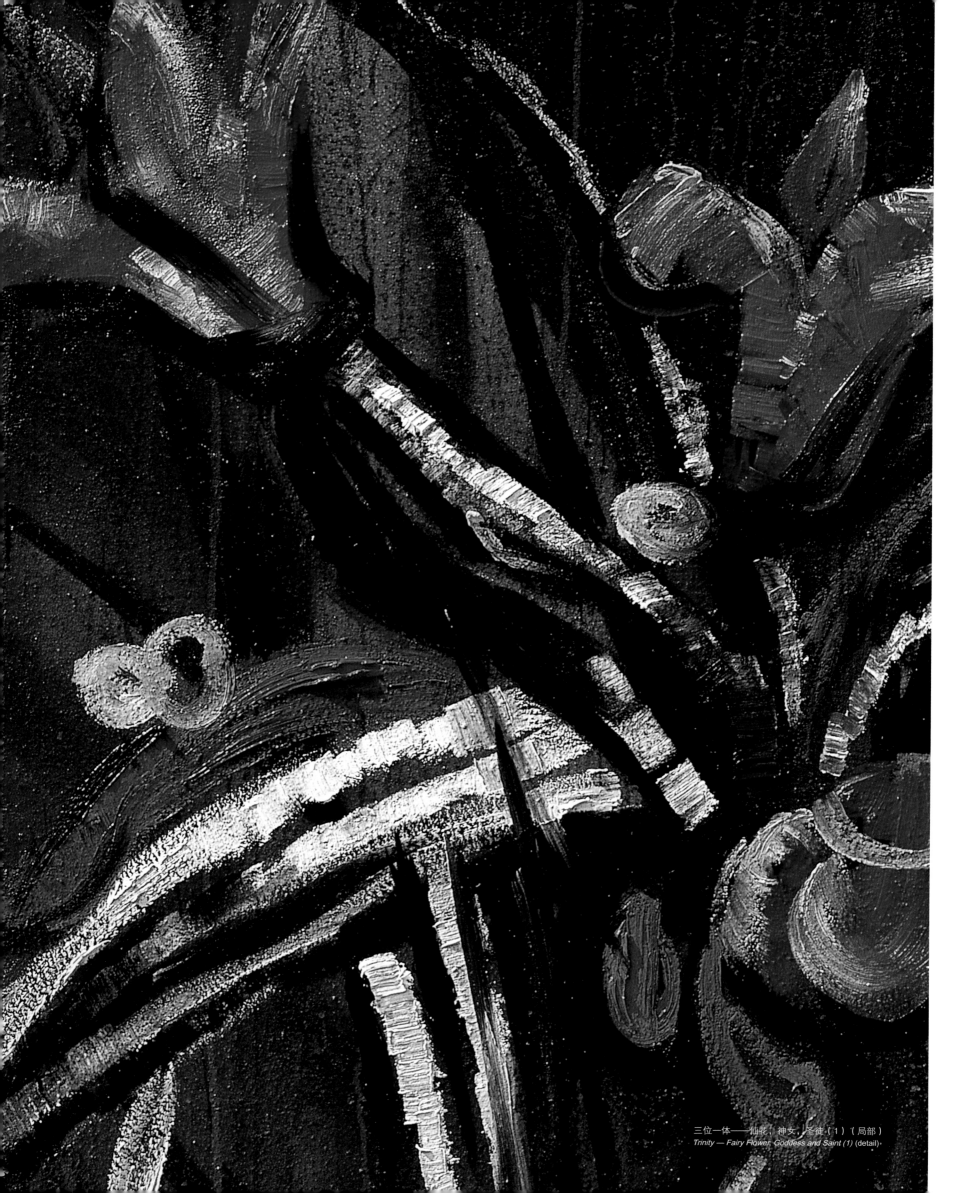

三位一体——仙花，神女，圣徒（1）（局部）
Trinity — Fairy Flower, Goddess and Saint (1) (detail)

三位一体——仙花，神女，圣徒（3）（局部）
Trinity — Fairy Flower, Goddess and Saint (3) (detail)

白月（1），2010，布上油彩、丙烯、大漆，206 × 163cm
White Moon (1), 2010, oil, acrylics and lacquer on canvas, 206 × 163 cm

白月（2），2010，布上油彩、丙烯、大漆，206 × 163cm
White Moon (2), 2010, oil, acrylics and lacquer on canvas, 206 × 163 cm

白月（3），2010，布上油彩、丙烯、大漆，206 × 163cm
White Moon (3), 2010, oil, acrylics and lacquer on canvas, 206 × 163 cm

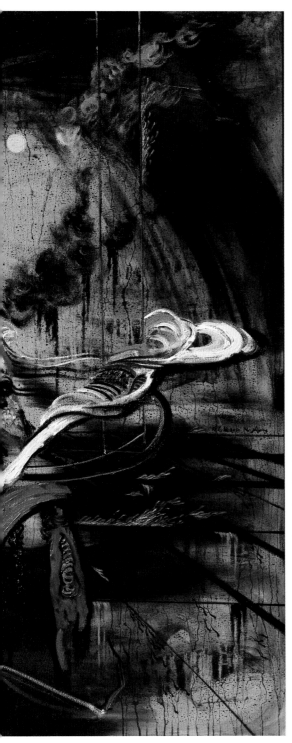

胡志颖的作品形式新颖、含义多元而蕴涵着永恒、庄严之美，从而构筑了一种"高贵的世界"（马尔库塞语），十分难得。他的艺术就是他自己的性灵独白。

——青 宇

With their novel style, diversified implications and eternal and imposing beauty, Hu Zhiying's works, very valuable, constitute a "noble world" (Herbert Marcuse). His art is a monologue of his own soul.

— Qing Yu

白月（1）（局部）
White Moon (1) (detail)

白月（3）（局部）
White Moon (3) (detail)

白月（2）（局部）
White Moon (2) (detail)

正如生命的本质没有边界一样，艺术形式的变化也无以穷尽，前一个浪潮退了下去，后一个浪潮又冲了上来，而在每一个浪潮上面都漂浮着某种需要解决的新问题。艺术家正是以他自由的创造力，沉湎于一切新形式之中，体验着人类独特的精神境界。

——胡志颖

Just as life is boundless in essence, the variation of art forms is limitless. When one wave recedes, another rolls forward, and on each wave floats a new problem needing to be resolved. It is with his free creativity that the artist is intoxicated with all the new forms,

中国画家胡志颖以培根赢得声望

埃德・麦科马克

纵览艺术史，或者有意地采用别人的风格的种种方面，或者完全临摹他们的作品，以赞扬别的艺术家，这在艺术家中蔚为风气（马奈就曾借用拉斐尔的整幅构图，而毕加索对鲁本斯和委拉斯贵支的崇敬也众所周知）。

在中国，传统的水墨画家学习描绘自然的种种元素的程式，靠的是临摹一本入门教材中的范图，这本教材名为《芥子园画谱》。在那里，模仿另一名艺术家的作品就是给予他或她一种最高的荣誉。然而，在西方，20世纪80年代挪用主义运动（艺术家精确地复制其他艺术家的作品，并公然作为自己的作品展出）的出现却引起了相当大的争议。

上述这一切使我们想到杰出的中国当代画家胡志颖的情况，其强有力的系列作品《重造培根》在他于纽约曼哈顿西二十五街511号国际美术馆举办的展览中展出，展览日期为2009年1月2日至31日（开幕酒会：1月8日，晚上6时至8时）。（图1，2）

展览还包括题为《天文》和《文字》的巨幅混合媒介绘画，使用的是一种与大卫・沙利（David Salle）相似的分层叠加的后现代手法，志颖将用精致的线条画成的树枝与岩石的形象叠加在以西方风格绘制的大幅半抽象风景画上，那些树枝与岩石的形象显然是用银色漆料临自《芥子园画谱》。犹如鬼斧神工般的重叠抄本，这些传统的中国水墨画的痕迹，似乎对影响问题、模仿问题和东西方对独创性看法的差异问题做出挖苦的评论。而在这样做的时候，它们使人们对这位极具天赋的中国画家对著名的英国画家弗朗西斯・培根（Francis Bacon）的作品的具有高度独创性的诠释有了心理上的准备。

培根本人就是一名伟大的模仿者，他不仅模仿埃德沃德・迈布里奇（Eadweard Muybridge）裸体摔跤手的动态照片，而且也模仿更早的画家。凡是熟悉他的作品的人，对此都不会感到新鲜。他所画的尖叫的教皇毕竟直接源于培根所模仿的肖像画《教皇英诺森十世》，对形象作了奇异的变形，将比真人更美的牧师肖像变为恶魔般的怪物的形象。

了解了这些情况，现在人们就可以用不那样带批判性的眼光来看待胡志颖对培根的另一幅画的"重造"了，这位英国艺术家是根据迈布里奇的一幅裸体摔跤手的照片绘制这幅画的（将他们置于床上，以使形象更具性的暗示意味）。在这样做的过程中，人们就会认识到，志颖实际上对最初的形象比培根做了更大的变动，将两个人物都画成蓝色而不是肉色，并使其中的一个人看上去确然无疑地是个女性（尽管那刚劲有力的表现主义的笔触使两个形象都成为半抽象的）。但是，其中最大的变化是一名美女的硕大无朋，她在头顶与乳房下裁切，守候在两个扭成一团的人体之后。这个形象尽管画得更模糊，但更写实，她暗示了对一次色情艳遇，对早已消逝的爱的场景的虚幻记忆。放在大的背景中看，这个形象明显地不协调，因为女性形象在培根的作品中只是很少出现，而且从来不像这个形象一样美。

在展览中，这幅画夹在另外两大幅画之间，构成一幅三联画，培根也常常偏爱这种格局。然而，尽管另外的两幅画也带有培根式视觉形式语汇，它们的具体来源却不那样容易辨析。因为胡志颖对两幅画中的形象都进行了比培根通常所做的更大的意象性解构，结果形成了这样一种构图，甚至尽管保留了培根的整体的构图冲击力和基调，实际上却似乎引用了朱利安・施纳贝尔（Julian Schnabel）的抽象性的某些方面。

因此，通过他自己的绘画性的阐释，志颖使我们对培根即使不是在题材上也是在形式、戏剧性和表现技巧等方面如何影响了施纳贝尔的问题有了饶有趣味的了解。但是，他自己对这位英国画家的意象所做的变形以其杰出的流畅性而更加有趣，中央的具有象征性的暗示性形体强有力地变形为蜿蜒的生物形态的团簇，以大片大片火红的貌似抽象表现主义的笔触为衬托，人们从画前向后退时，扭曲的培根式的面孔便从这些笔触中浮现出来。

在这组壮观的三联画中，志颖赞扬了培根，同时又创造了某种新颖的、十分令人兴奋的事物，正如他在对《绘画1964年》所作的另一个富于想象力的抽象的"再造"中所做的那样，那是一幅开创性的画，将从脊骨一分两半的牛的躯体与半掩在一把黑伞下的邪恶的、殡葬业者般的人物相并置，培根以此画赢得了早期的声望（此画本身是苏丁[Soutine]的血淋淋的表现主义的畜体与文艺复兴时期的大师马萨乔[Masaccio]的湿壁画《三位一体》的混合物）。

胡志颖生活在中国广州，任教于华南师范大学美术学院，他以其在国际美术馆举办的这次展览对多元文化的潮流作出重要的说明，在这股潮流中，将往昔、现今和未来的画家们联系在一起的影响、灵感与创新相交融。随着北京迅速成为世界当代艺术重镇之一，胡志颖作为国际艺术明星赢得声望似乎只是个时间问题。

（原载《画廊与工作室》2008年11/12月号与2009年1月号合刊，纽约）

Chinese Painter Hu Zhiying Makes His Bones with Bacon

By Ed McCormack

Down through art history it has been common practice for artists to pay tribute to other artists by cither deliberately adopting aspects of each others' style or copying their works outright (Manet once borrowed an entire composition from Raphael and we're all familiar with Picasso's homage to Rubens and Velazquez.)

In China, where traditional ink painters learn the conventions for depicting various elements of nature by copying the examples in an instruction primer called *The Mustard Seed Manual*, to copy another artist's work is to confer on him or her the highest kind of honor. In the west, however, the advent of the Appropriation Movement (artists making exact duplicate of works by other artists and blatantly exhibiting them as their own) caused considerable controversy in the 1980s.

All of which brings us to the case of Hu Zhiying, a distinguished contemporary Chinese painter whose powerful series *Remake Bacon*, is on view in his exhibition at World Fine Art Gallery, 511 West 25th Street, from January 2 through 31, 2009 (Reception: January 8, 6 to 8pm.) (Fig. 1, Fig. 2)

The exhibition also includes large mixed media paintings titled *Astronomy* and *Characters*, in which, working in a layered postmodern manner akin to David Salle, Zhiying superimposes delicate linear images of tree limbs and rocks apparently copied in white paint from *The Mustard Seed Manua*l over large semiabstract landscapes painted in the Western manner. Like ghostly palimpsests, these vestiges of traditional Chinese ink painting seem to comment wryly on issues of influence, copying, and the difference between how originality is viewed in the East and the West. And in doing so, they prime one's mind for this immensely gifted Chinese painter's highly original take on the work of the famous British painter Francis Bacon.

It should be news to no one familiar with his work that Bacon himself was a great copier, not only of Eadweard Muybridge's motion photographs of naked wrestlers, but of earlier painters as well. His paintings of screaming popes, after all, derived directly from portrait *Pope Innocent X* that Bacon copied, subjecting the image to grotesque distortions, transforming a flattering clerical likeness into an image of demonic monster.

Armed with this information, one can now look at Hu Zhiying's "remakes" of another painting by Bacon that the British artist based on one of Muybridge's photograph's of naked wrestlers (placing them on a bed to make the image more sexually suggestive) with a less judgmental eye. And in doing so, one may realize that Zhiying actually transforms the original image even more than Bacon did, making both of the figures blue rather than flesh-colored and making one of them appear decidedly feminine (despite the vigorous expressionist strokes that render both semi-abstract). But the biggest change of all is the huge of a beautiful woman, cropped at the top of the head and below the breasts, hovering behind the two merged bodies. Painted more realistically, albeit more faintly, she suggests the phantom memory of an erotic encounter, a haunting vision of love long gone. In context, this image is strikingly incongruous, since female figures appear only rarely in Bacon's oeuvre, and are never beautiful like this one.

In the exhibition, this painting is bracketed between two other large canvases to form a triptych, a configuration that Bacon himself often favored. However, while the other two canvases also partake of a Baconesque visual vocabulary of forms, their specific sources are not as readily discernible. For Hu Zhiying has subjected the figures in both canvases to considerably more imagistic deconstruction than Bacon usually did, creating a composition that, in fact, appears to reference certain aspects of Julian Schnabel's abstractions even while retaining the overall compositional thrust and mood of Bacon.

Thus, through his own painterly articulation, Zhiying gives us an interesting insight as to how Bacon influenced Schnabel in terms of form, drama, and showmanship, if not in subject matter. But his own transmutations of the British painter's imagery are even more interesting for their brilliant fluidity, with the central figuratively allusive forms metamorphosing muscularly into sinuous biomorphic clusters set against expanses of fiery red seemingly Abstract Expressionist brushwork from which distorted Baconish faces emerge when one steps back from the canvas.

In this stately triptych, Zhiying pays tribute to Bacon while creating something new and quite sensational, just as he does in another imaginatively abstracted "remake" of *Painting 1964*, the seminal picture juxtaposing sides of beef with a sinister mortician-like figure half-hidden under a black umbrella with which Bacon made a early reputation (itself an amalgam of Soutine's bloody Expressionist carcasses and the Renaissance master Masaccio's fresco of *the Trinity*).

With this exhibition at World Fine Art Gallery, Hu Zhiying, who lives in Guangzhou, China, and teaches at the College of Fine Arts of South China Normal University, makes a major statement about the multicultural currents of cross-fertilization of influence, inspiration and innovation that unite painters of the past, present, and future. With Beijing fast becoming one of the major contemporary art capitals of the world, it seems only a matter of time before he makes his bones as an international art star.

(*Gallery & Studio,* Nov/Dec 2008-Jan 2009, New York)

（图1）胡志颖2009年纽约展览
(Fig. 1) Hu Zhiying's Exhibition in New York in 2009

（图2）胡志颖2009年纽约展览
(Fig. 2) Hu Zhiying's Exhibition in New York in 2009

胡志颖艺术中形式的含义、个人宗教与培根问题

地点：北京798艺术区
时间：2009年7月12日
人物：罗宾·佩卡姆（简称"罗"）
　　　胡志颖（简称"胡"）

罗：形式上，您最近的作品（图1，2）与早期的技术很成熟的绘画（图3）之间存在着很大的区别。画早期那些作品的时候是什么样的状态？当时认为自己是当代艺术家吗？跟80年代的'85新潮、星星画会、池社、厦门达达等趋势有没有交流？

胡：当时我就迷恋画画，并没有当代艺术家的概念。我的基本状态和观念历来都很个人化。我的基本点是个人决定论，而不是某一股潮流。尽管我的画风屡次改变，批评家们也无法将我的艺术归为任何一个流派。因为只有建立一个特殊的个体的个性的时候，才能真正证明你作为一个中国人，或者德国人、法国人是有价值的。真正富于力量的"中国气派"，仰仗于艺术创造的主体的自信——吸纳东西方元素的自决、建立作品中自我精神的主宰、形式相比较于两个纬度——中国传统艺术和西方现代艺术——上所表现出来的卓尔不群。

罗：您80年代绘画作品，另外几幅画在课本上的翻印图片（图4，5），这些作品是不是仅仅为了表现绘画技术而制作的？主题是怎么找的？主题很明显跟当时中国的情况没有直接的关系，有什么样的文化来源？

胡：我并没有刻意寻找题材，我不表现日常性和常规性的主题。我更希望作品有形式上力量，这样才有说服力。（图6）而且，这种说服力往往并不是广泛的，我相信中国古代那句话："阳春白雪，和者必寡"，也就是说，真正好的艺术接受的人是很少的。一般的社会现象总是大家喜欢围绕一种流行的东西，或者被多数人关注的东西所牵引。

罗：您有文学博士的学位，对吗？我最近在慢慢地开始看您的《文学彼岸性研究》。怎么想到对这种问题进行研究？与您在视觉艺术上的工作有没有关系？

胡：是的。《文学彼岸性研究》与其说是对中国古典文学终极问题的研究，还不如说更是关于中国某类古典文本我个人阅读经验的描述。这一经验产生于我少儿时代，这本书可以说是完成了我自少儿时代以来的一个梦想。显然，"文学彼岸性"是适合于文字表述的一个问题，因而与我的视觉艺术并无直接关系。如果把艺术作为图解一个哲学命题或者某种观念的话，这往往会导致视觉艺术的失败，或者说对视觉艺术而言没有太大的意义。其实这种东西应该是更深层的、某种潜在的、难以言说的影响，这样的情况才是比较好的。

罗：您怎么看您作为艺术教育者的角色？

胡：我觉得老师的作用更多的是启发学生，而不是简单地教学生怎么做或者形成什么样的观念。反而是要介绍古今中外更多的不同艺术流派，介绍文化现象的多元性，供学生进行自由选择。所以，我希望在教学中提供一种自由的空间——包括观念和技术上，给学生自主选择。

罗：您对宗教感兴趣吗？还是像培根一样，光对受到信仰与神话影响的人类行为感兴趣？跟暴力有没有关系？在您作品中，愉快与恐怖能否同时存在？

胡：我自己概念系统中的"个人宗教"很重要：个人宗教的主体体验到灵魂的内在力量只有作为个人的独立存在，才能走向灵魂的最深处，它的超然本质，实际上与宗教教义、宗

（图1）方程式之三，1996，布上综合媒介，200×180cm（见084页）
(Fig.1) *Equations III*, 1996, mixed media on canvas, 200×180 cm (see p. 084)

（图2）原子之三，1997，布上综合媒介，180×200cm（见094页）
(Fig. 2) *Atoms III*, 1997, mixed media on canvas, 180 × 200 cm (see p. 094)

（图3）古董，1987，布上油彩，111×89.7cm
(Fig. 3) *Antiques*, 1987, oil on canvas, 111 × 89.7 cm

（图4）盆中鱼，1980，纸上油彩，39.3×36.6cm
(Fig. 4) *Fish in the Basin*, 1980, oil on paper, 39.3 × 36.6 cm

（图5）生命世系图，1986，布上油彩，170×400cm（见203页）
(Fig. 5) *Life's Pedigrees Picture*, oil on canvas, 170 × 400 cm (see p. 203)

（图6）原子之四，1997，布上综合媒介，200×180cm（见096页）
(Fig. 6) *Atoms IV*, 1997, mixed media on canvas, 200 × 180 cm (see p. 096)

教活动、宗教规范这些后天行为根本上不是一回事。如果说宗教是用来抚慰心灵、表达苦恼或自谴心情的圣事，那么，个人宗教的表达则不受宗教制约以及与世俗道德判断无关，对灵魂深处隐秘语言本真、自然的表达。对于这至高无上的灵魂语言的态度使这一主体认为，这样做比宗教本身更自然和独到。宗教信仰是通过理性而不是通过灵魂的默示所得出的结果，真实而本然的个人宗教相形而卓然不群。我并没有在画中着意表现暴力，如果观众产生这种感觉也是自由的。就艺术而言，我认为愉快和恐怖可以当然地并存，尽管这不一定合乎理性认知的逻辑。

罗：我想对几幅画细读。在培根画中的故事层上，基座及家具对躯体起了很大的影响（图7，8）。另外，培根所画的支撑着躯体的曲线导致画中故事层因素与非故事层因素区别的瓦解。在您作品中，情况很不一样了。基座与构思还重要吗？好像是躯体对您比较重要。

胡：我对培根画中的有关故事并无兴趣，我自己更无意在画里面表现故事。躯干、怪异的生物造型、交错的骨架等等，更在形式意义上由我驾驭，而且，我相信形式本身就能激发出意义。我希望使得其中的含义模糊不清、能指范围更为广阔。此外，我的画面的背景不同于培根，我的背景广大、虚化、深沉；堆厚形成很强肌理技术语言也不同。我将东方虚化的幽冥意境和西方强调物质感的因素穿插在一起，造成一种无以名状的氛围。（图9）

罗：这里能看到的画跟原来的还不一样，培根后来改了一些地方。有一些元素被消除掉了，包括：花卉，山水，还有一个遥远的躯体。您在主要躯体旁边添加了另外一个躯体，是不是原来已经知道培根的第一个习作？躯体后面的红色黄色形状是什么东西，是山水的构架吗？（图10）

胡：我画中的背景是一组色情场面而不是山水，不过我并没有突出这一点，而是将其局部放大到产生某种抽象视觉效果。前景的怪异生物以及其他图像更多的是根据对画面形式——造型、色彩、空间的直觉而进行表现的，综合起来，是某种关于自己感觉、思维、认知的视觉形式的实现。

罗：培根在这幅画里面开始探索的主题与风格继续利用了一辈子，不过您好像是生涯已经相当发达的时候才开始探究。年龄与经历跟您的重新解读方式有什么关系？

胡：虽然知道培根的人很多，但我相信真正能感受培根里面的精神的人是非常少的，所以受培根影响的艺术家反而很少。我对培根的借鉴是来自我自己的一种感受，我一直对一些神秘、怪异、幽冥的东西有一种强烈的兴趣和表达欲望。然后这些东西和自己长期积累的东西相碰撞，形成这样一种表达方式。

罗：对培根来说，躯体的肉体性很重要，尤其是它的嘴巴。在您作品中，这个躯体好像变得更加肉体，更有折磨的感觉。但是具体的身体结构有点变化：从躯体出来的尖状物是不是带有新的含义？

胡：我更注重的是作品本身的形式，比如从躯体出来的尖状物我并没有清晰具体的所指。但作品无论形式还是内涵都与培根是不同的，创作方法论也不一样。其实，有些东西在一些很小的甚至一些看似不重要的方面做出改变的时候，实际上已经发生了很大的乃至于根本的变化。从历史上看，塞尚借鉴毕萨罗就是很好的例子，塞尚认为自己永远不可能超越毕萨罗，但实际上，塞尚对毕萨罗的些微改变——看似些微改变，已经发生了根本性的变化，乃至划时代的变革。

（原载《世界文化》2010年第九期，世界文化杂志社）

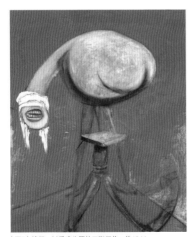 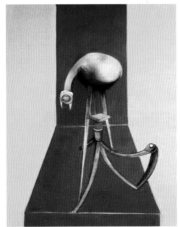

（图7）培根，以受难为题的三张习作，约1944
(Fig. 7) Bacon, *Three Studies for figures at the Base of a Crucifixion ca*, 1944

（图8）培根，1944，三联画第二版，1988
(Fig. 8) Bacon, *Second Version of Triptych, 1944*, 1988

（图9）重造培根——蝙蝠与玫瑰（1），2004–2005 布上油彩、丙烯、大漆，196×153cm（见148页）
(Fig. 9) *Remake Bacon — Bat and Rose (1)*, 2004-2005, oil, acrylic, lacquer on canvas, 196 × 153 cm (see p. 148)

（图10）培根梦与性爱（3），2007，布上油彩、丙烯、大漆，192×153 cm（见163页）
(Fig. 10) *Bacon's Dream and Sex (3)*, 2007, oil, acrylic, lacquer on canvas, 192 × 153 cm (see p163)

Meaning of Forms, Personal Religion and Issues about Francis Bacon in Hu Zhiying's Art: An Interview

Interviewee: Hu Zhiying (H for short)
Interviewer: Robin Peckham (R for short)
Date: July 12, 2009
Place: Beijing 798 Art Zone

R: There is a huge stylistic difference between your early paintings, which are obviously technically proficient (Fig. 3), and your more recent work (Fig. 1, Fig. 2). How did you see your position as an artist in those early works? Would you consider yourself a contemporary artist at that time? Were you in dialogue with movements like the '85 New Wave, the Stars, Pond Collective, Xiamen Dada, or anything like that?

H: I merely took a passionate interest in producing paintings at that time, without any idea of being a contemporary artist. My basic state and ideas are always considerably individualized. My basic point is personal determinism rather than a certain tide. Although my style of painting changes time and again, critics are unable to locate my art in any school. For only when your specific individuality has formed can your value as a Chinese, a German or a French be truly proved. Truly powerful "Chinese manner" depends on the confidence of the subject of artistic creation: self-determination in absorbing Eastern and Western elements, domination in establishing self-spirit in the works, and excellence of the form manifested in comparison with two latitudes — Chinese traditional art and Western modern art.

R: Your images of work from the early 1980s (Fig. 4, Fig. 5), and your a reproduction of their reproduction in a textbook, were these paintings executed purely for their technical value? How did you choose the material? Where are your cultural influences coming from?

H: I do not look for subject matters intentionally, and I do not depict every-day and conventional themes. I hope my works are powerful in terms of form so that they may be convincing. (Fig. 6) And what is more, they often may not be convincing to the large audience, for I believe in the ancient Chinese saying: "A highbrow tune is never popular." That is to say, truly good art is accepted only by a few. It is a general social phenomenon that people like to follow something in vogue or are under the sway of something most people pay close attention to.

R: You have a doctorate in literature, is that correct? I've been reading your book *On the Paramitality in Literature*. Why did you decide to research this kind of thing? How is this related to your practice as a visual artist?

H: Yes. *On the Paramitality in Literature* is not so much a research about the ultimate problems of Chinese classical literature as a description of my personal reading experience of certain kinds of Chinese classical texts. This experience originated from my boyhood, and this book can be said to have realized a dream I have cherished since my boyhood. It is obvious that the Paramitality in literature is a topic suitable to be expounded in textual form, therefore it has no direct relation with my visual art. Trying to illustrate a philosophical proposition or an idea tends to result in the failure of visual art, or is of no great significance to visual art. In fact, it is better to say that it is a matter of profound, latent and indescribable influence.

R: How do you see your role as an art educator?

H: I think the more proper role of a teacher lies in enlightening the students instead of simply telling them what to do or what ideas to form. He should give an account of more and different art schools in modern or ancient times, in China or elsewhere, and diverse cultural phenomena, so that the students may make free choice. Therefore, I hope, in our teaching, we can provide a free space — both ideological and technical — where the students may make their own choice.

R: Are you interested in religion, or are you, like Bacon, more interested in the idea of human behavior as influenced by belief and mythology? How does violence figure into this equation? Are pleasure and horror both present here?

H: The "personal religion" in my own conceptual system is very important. The subject who believes in personal religion realizes that only when the internal power of the soul is a personal independent existence can it penetrate into the utmost depth of the soul. Being detached in essence, this personal religion is completely different from such acquired things as religious doctrines, religious activities and religious norms. If religion is something sacred serving to console one's mind and express one's worry or self-reproach, then what is expressed in personal religion is not restrained by religion and has nothing to do with secular moral judgment. It is a sincere and natural expression of the secret language in the depth of one's soul. The attitude to this supreme language of the soul makes the subject think that to do so is more natural and original than religion itself. Religious belief is the result obtained through reason rather than tacit revelation of the soul, and in comparison, the true and natural personal religion is pre-eminent. I have not expressed violence intentionally in my paintings, but the beholders have the freedom to think so. As far as art is concerned, I think that pleasure and terror can certainly coexist, though this may not necessarily conform to the logic of reasonable cognition.

R: Now I'd like to do a close reading of several images. (Fig. 7, Fig. 8) The pedestals and furniture play an important role in terms of diegetic framing of the figures. There may even be a lapse between the diegetic and non-diegetic worlds with the converging lines that support the figures. In your work this shifts dramatically. Have they lost some importance to you? You seem to be concentrating on the figure itself.

H: I am not interested in related stories in Bacon's paintings, let alone try to depict stories in my paintings. figures, grotesque creatures, interlaced skeletons, etc., are all in my control in the sense of form, and I believe that forms themselves can generate meanings. I hope to make the meaning obscure and the range of signifier broader. In addition, the backgrounds of my paintings are different from those of Bacon's. They are extensive, indistinct and dark. Piling of colors results in strong textures and the technical language is also different from Bacon's. I have created an aura beyond description by interweaving together indistinct and gloomy ambiance of the East and elements of the West emphasizing material sense. (Fig. 9)

R: Bacon had erased certain elements from his initial composition: flowers, something of a landscape, and a figure in the distance. Were you aware of this when you added a rather prominent figure behind the main figure? What are the red and yellow shapes behind the main figure — are they a type of landscape environment? (Fig. 10)

H: In the background of my painting is not landscape but a group of erotic scenes. But I didn't give prominence to them. Instead, I enlarged a part to achieve some abstract visual effect. The grotesque creature in the foreground and other images were depicted rather according to my intuition about the forms, that is, shapes, colors, and space. In sum, this painting is an embodiment of my feeling, thought and understanding in visual form.

R: The themes and styles Bacon introduced in these paintings were formative for the rest of his career, yet you seem to pick them up well into your own career. What does age or experience have to do with your reinterpretation?

H: Although lots of people know of Bacon, I believe that only a few can truly comprehend his spirit, and therefore very few artists are influenced by him. The reason why I draw on Bacon's art is that I am always intensely interested in mysterious, grotesque and gloomy things and have a strong desire to depict them. Then the collision of such things with what I have accumulated in a long period results in such a mode of expression.

R: The physicality of the creature — especially its mouth — was very important to Bacon. It seems even more tortured, even more of a body in your work. But it seems to have some added anatomy: what is the large spike emerging from the figure?

H: I lay more stress on the form of the works themselves. For instance, such things as the large spike emerging from the figure have no definite or concrete reference. However, my works are different from Bacon's in both form and connotation, and we have different methodologies of creation. As a matter of fact, when things are changed in some small or even unimportant aspects seemingly, enormous or even fundamental changes have actually taken place. The using of Pissarro's art for reference by Cézanne is a good example in history. Cézanne thought that he could never surpass Pissarro, but in fact, though Cézanne had made some slight changes, seemingly slight changes, to Pissarro's style, fundamental changes, or even epoch-making changes, had already taken place.

(Originally published in the 9th issue of *World Culture* in 2010, World Culture Magazine)

胡志颖的崇高美学

鲍　栋

　　胡志颖提供给我们的并不是那些不言自明，一望便知的东西，尽管从九十年代以来，我们眼前就一直充斥着这样的东西。实际上，对中国当代艺术三十年的叙述，自始至终都没有脱离过社会决定论的底色，因此，"关怀社会"、"反映现实"、"立足当下"等等这些观念一直是中国当代艺术中的强势话语，不管是对于创作实践还是理论批评。这种社会决定论，体现为现实主义的文艺观念，虽然，自伤痕美术以来，社会主义现实主义的权威就受到了挑战，但是现实主义的观念本身依然内在地统治着人们的大脑，伤痕美术、乡土绘画，乃至90年代的玩世现实主义都属于现实主义的美学框架，而政治波普、艳俗艺术以及卡通绘画的背后，也依然是一种政治、经济的社会叙事，所以本质上还是现实主义的变种。

　　也正是这些艺术风格与流派相对获得了本土及国际市场的认同，而被当成了所谓"中国当代艺术"的代表。究其历史原因，除了后殖民状况所带来的自我他者化之外，现实主义的观念在中国深入人心的程度也是不能被忽视的。当大部分观众依然处于现实主义的美学制度之中的时候，那些或隐或显的现实主义作品受到欢迎就是自然而然的了，因为，它们一望便知，让人们觉得毫无困难，让人们可以便利地获得一种关于中国社会最新事态与心态的描述，进而能够获得了一种假想的在场感。而现实主义——观念或手法——却是不言自明的，或者说，是不被察觉的，因为它就像是眼镜，戴着眼镜的人是无法看见眼镜的，而他们所看见的一切却已被眼镜所定义。

　　在这种现实主义的眼镜下，像胡志颖这样的艺术家是很难被看见的，他所描述的"景象"与中国社会并没有直接的，或者说，现实主义式的联系。甚至，他的作品是不考虑"现实"这个概念的，对于胡志颖来说，"现实"只不过是"幻象"的另一种说法，艺术真正要抵达的是彼岸性——这个来自于康德哲学的术语暗示了那些无法被认识的自在之物的存在，因而提供给我们了一个超越性的视点，使我们获得了从经验世界，即现象界中抽身离开的可能。

　　从一开始，胡志颖面对的就是这样一种可能，当1978年他还在江西师范学院学美术的时候，就已经通过《美术丛刊》、《外国美术资料》（即后来的《美术译丛》）、《世界美术》等刊物受到了超现实主义的影响，因此，在他1980年的作品中，现实主义的美学就已经被抛弃了。虽然这幅《无题》的绘画中依然有叙述，但已不是那些典型人物、典型环境、典型情节的现实主义叙述模式，而是采用了象征主义的手法，把具体的时间与空间关系打破，用形象之间的象征关系来叙述生命的成长过程，并以此隐喻了历史的发展。[1]（图1）值得一提的是，在这幅作品中已经包含了贯穿了八十年代的文化反思主题，而这个主题将伴随着胡志颖直到九十年代与现在。

　　即便是在他讴歌改革开放的作品《万世之业》（1984）中，（图2）这种象征主义的手法也很明显，而与当时官方美术中的直接描绘新时期建设成果绘画拉开了距离，这说明了，胡志颖的艺术实践从一开始就是中国当代艺术的一个部分，如果我们把中国当代艺术的发生底线设立为反对官方艺术样式的话。随着'85美术运动的开始，胡志颖所受到的超现实主义影响更加显露，在1986年的《生命世系图》中，（图3）虽然"生命"的文化反思主题没有变化，但是绘画中的形象关系已不再属于象征主义的隐喻套式，而出现了真正属于超现实主义的蒙太奇手法。但是，与1985年张群、孟禄丁的《在新时代——亚当与夏娃的启示》，以及"南京青年艺术周·大型现代艺术展"中杨迎生、任戎、徐一晖等人的超现实主义倾向的作品所受到的关注相比，胡志颖的这些绘画并未获得广泛的关注，甚至他的《生命世系图》一直未能获得公开展示的机会。这与他当时地处江西的偏僻小城有关，也与他执拗、孤僻的性

（图1）无题，1980，布上油彩，玻璃，沙砾，拼贴，200×135cm
(Fig. 1) *Untitled*, 1980, oil, glass, grit and collage on canvas, 200 × 135 cm

（图2）万世之业，1984，布上油彩，200×200cm
(Fig. 2) *An Undertaking for All Ages*, oil on canvas, 200 × 200 cm

格有关，尤其是性格原因，因为，他在1987年考上广州美院国画专业研究生之后创作的水墨实验作品也并未获得应有的关注。

胡志颖的艺术观念正是在他研究生时代成型的，可以概括为他硕士论文的主题《艺术无常论》，其核心是一种建立在自由主义思想基础之上的文化相对主义。在八十年代末及九十年代之初，意识形态左倾回潮的背景下，胡的遭遇可想而知，他的论文因不符合"马克思主义"而没有获得正式答辩的机会。

在这里，胡志颖提供了一个重新反思八十年代与九十年代之间艺术史转折的一个契机。现有的中国当代艺术史的书写基本是把这一转折描述为人文理想主义的降格与冷漠的现实主义（新生代）、自我解嘲的现实主义（玩世现实主义）与政治反讽的后现代主义（政治波普），这样一种艺术史叙述还可以延伸到九十年代末文化反讽的后现代主义（艳俗艺术）、感伤的现实主义（新伤痕与青春残酷绘画），以及二十一世纪初出现的时尚现实主义（新卡通艺术）。简言之，这是一条以现实主义为基底的叙述，艺术被理解为对社会现实——迎奉或反讽的——态度，即使是反对这一叙述的人，也只大都是站在这一现实主义基底的另一种立场上，如批判前者的犬儒与媚俗，只是价值观的差异，而没有表征观念上的不同。

但是，胡志颖的艺术观念与实践无法被纳入到这样的艺术史叙述中，他1989年创作的水墨实验作品就已经开始了流行图像的挪用，在《透视》这件作品中就出现了好莱坞电影《星球大战》中的太空战机，但是胡志颖并不是用它们表达某种政治态度或者反映某种社会现实。[2] 在胡志颖的这一系列及以后的作品中，艺术与社会现实并无直接的关联，流行图像在这里只属于符号世界，它们与几何形体、汉字、字母、空间及"水墨"本身构成了一个内部碎化的自足体，换句话说，它们只是形式。在这个意义上，胡志颖是一位坚定的形式主义者。

但他并不是吴冠中那种形式装饰主义者，胡志颖并没有把形式依附在某种审美经验的俗套上，而是始终强调形式的绝对性，因此，他把形式上升为康德哲学中的先验形式。在《水墨语言的先天综合性》一文中，他把水墨画的创作规范为先天"水墨语言"的综合判断，即是把"水墨语言"上升为一种先天结构，而具体的水墨画只不过是这一先天结构的演绎。[3] 暂且不论胡志颖对康德的这些概念范畴的运用是否合理，就其把形式主义问题追溯到康德哲学的思路而言，无疑是深刻的，他抓住了形式主义的要害。并且，这也避免了那种把"水墨"放到文化身份问题中去讨论的文化保守主义思路，提供了一个开放地面对"水墨"问题的普遍性视角。

他的这一思路同样也可以运用到其他的艺术媒介与类型上，实际上也正是如此，在九十年代初开始的绘画实验中，他扩展了媒材的范围，如金粉、银粉、大漆、砚砆这类中国传统工艺美术中的材料。另一方面，他却收拢了他的"符号世界"，在九十年代初的一系列作品中，大量出现的是宋代山水风格的图像碎片，它们与来自西方文化的绘画及摄影图像发生穿插、叠印与对比，形成了一种迷离的视觉场域。与此同时，一种样式主义的因素出现了，即强化某种既定的风格，在胡志颖的这些作品中，表现为对宋代山水风格的强调，尤其是对笔法本身的炫耀，于是，风格被从"内容"上剥离了下来，成为了一种纯粹的风格化的形式，这一特征一直延伸到了胡志颖2000年之后的"重造培根"系列，促成了一种矫饰的培根风格。

但是形式的背后是不可能没有其内容的，胡志颖对纯粹形式的强调——用利奥塔的话来说——是为了表现某种"不可表现之物"，亦可以理解为前文所述的"彼岸性"。"彼岸性"是胡志颖的一个关键概念，他2002年的博士论文《文学彼岸性研究》即是以这个词为基础的中国古典文学美学研究，虽然这篇论文研究的是文学，但足以说明他的艺术观念。在康德的哲学体系中，"彼岸性"是指处于认识能力之外的物自体，对于主体来说，审美活动一旦企图触及这种"彼岸性"，即认识活动一旦要去认识不可认识之物，那么主体就会意识到其界限，进而激发出崇高感。崇高一直是属于古典美学的范畴，但是利奥塔则在先锋派的语境中，重新建立了崇高的美学价值，他把"崇高"从康德的主体哲学中抽取了出来，认为崇高即是对某种绝对之物的意识，崇高即意味着有不可表现之物存在。[4]

胡志颖对"彼岸性"的强调就属于这种崇高美学。在他的绘画实践中，这种崇高美学体现为两个截然相反的维度：一方面他试图呈现某种绝对的精神性，把既定的符号、图像系统，以及背后的意义系统视为幻象而彻底打碎，以表征某种精神本体的不可表征性；另一方面，则是投身到彻底的物质性层面，用材料（媒介的物性）、笔触（身体的物性）来建立一种意义的不透明性，以抵抗世俗精神的入侵，见证着不可表征性本身。值得一提的是，利奥塔已经对这两种崇高做出了划分，前者是以超现实主义为代表，后者以抽象表现主义为代表——实际上，胡志颖不正是试图把这两者结合起来吗？

不管胡志颖是否已经达到他的目标，也不管他在这一目标下的实践是否有意义，问题是，我们所说的"中国当代艺术"该如何面对他以及其它类似的艺术实践，而在我们的中国当代艺术史叙述中，又如何去讲述这样一条线索。

注释：
① 有趣的是，虽然当时很多人都受到了超现实主义的影响，但这种通过观摩画册而带来的影响只能停留在视觉语言上，因此，达利的具象的超现实主义被风 格化后，与当时的文化反思主题结合在了一起，最终形成的是一种象征主义的手法。
② 实际上，政治波普也并没有表达一种政治态度，只是被西方，进而被我们解读为一种政治态度。
③ 参胡志颖：《水墨语言的先天综合性》，《国画家》，2000年，04期，中国美术家协会。
④ 参利奥塔：《非人》，罗国祥译，商务印书馆，2000年版，131-143页。

（原载《在幻象锁链的彼岸——胡志颖绘画作品1989-2009》，中国环球文化出版社，2010）

The Sublime Aesthetics of Hu Zhiying

By Bao Dong

What Hu Zhiying has provided us with are not those self-evident things, although from the 1990s onward, we are always facing such kind of things. In fact, the narrative of the three decades of Chinese contemporary art has never got rid of the basic tone of social determinism; therefore, concepts like "being concerned about the society", "reflecting reality" and "basing ourselves on present times" have always been dominant discourses in Chinese contemporary art, both in practice of creation and theoretical criticism. This social determinism comes from the vulgar Marxism that began to prevail in China in 1949 with realistic concepts of art and literary as its embodiment. Although the authority of Socialist Realism has been challenged since the appearance of Scar Art, the concept of Realism itself is still dominating people's mind inherently. Scar Art, Local Painting as well as Cynical Realism of the1990s all belong to the aesthetic framework of Realism, while behind Political Pop, Gaudy Art and Cartoon Painting is still a kind of social narrative of politics and economy, and therefore they are essentially still varieties of Realism.

It is these artistic styles and schools that are relatively acknowledged by native and international markets and are regarded as representatives of so-called "Chinese contemporary art". Among its historical causes, besides the otherness of self brought about by the post-colonial situation, the extent to which the realist concept has taken root in the hearts of the people in China is also not negligible. When most audiences are still in the aesthetic system of realism, it is natural that those obscure or obvious realistic works are warmly received. For, understandable at a glance without any difficulty, they allow people to acquire conveniently a description of the latest state of affairs and state of mind in Chinese society and to acquire further an imaginary sense of presence. Yet realism — its concept or techniques — is self-evident, or in other words, unperceivable. It is like spectacles. People wearing spectacles cannot see them, and all that they have seen have already been defined by the spectacles.

Through these spectacles of realism, artists like Hu Zhiying can hardly be seen, for the "scenes" he has depicted have no direct or realistic link with Chinese society. The concept of "reality" is even not considered in his works. For Hu Zhiying, "reality" is nothing but another word for "illusion", and the true destination of art is Paramitality (Jenseitigkeit). The term that comes from Kantian Philosophy implies the existence of the unknowable thing-in-itself and thus provides us with a transcendent viewpoint and makes it possible for us to get away from the world of experience, i.e., the phenomenal world.

Hu Zhiying faced such a possibility from the very beginning. As early as 1978 when he was studying art at Jiangxi Normal College, he was already influenced by Surrealism through such periodicals as *Fine Art Series*, *Selected Data of Foreign Art* (its name was later changed into *Fine Art Translations*) and *World Art*; therefore the realistic aesthetics was already discarded in his works of 1980. Although narratives still exist in the painting *Untitled*, they no longer belong to the realistic mode of narrative of typical characters, typical circumstances and typical plots. Instead, adopting the symbolist method, the artist breaks the concrete relation of time and space and narrates the process of growth of life as a metaphor of the development of history using the symbolic relation between images. [1] (Fig. 1) It is worth mentioning that the theme of cultural reflection that dominated throughout the 1980s is already contained in this painting, and this theme would accompany Hu Zhiying up to the 1990s and today.

This symbolic method is obvious even in his *An Undertaking for All Ages* (1984), (Fig. 2) a painting eulogizing the reform and opening-up. It distances the painting from those depicting directly construction achievements of the New Period in the office art at that time. This shows that the artistic practice of Hu Zhiying is part of Chinese contemporary art from the very beginning, if we take the anti-official mode of art as the base line of Chinese contemporary art. With the beginning of the '85 Art Movement, the influence of Surrealism upon Hu Zhiying was even more obvious. In his *Life's Pedigrees Picture* of 1986, (Fig. 3) though there is no change in the theme of cultural reflection on life, the relations between images in the painting no longer belong to the metaphorical convention of symbolism and montage is used which belongs truly to surrealism. However, compared with Zhang Qun and Meng Luding's *In the New Age — Inspiration from Adam and Eva* of 1985 and works by Yang Yingsheng, Ren Rong, Xu Yihui and others with a tendency of surrealism shown at Nanjing Youth Art Week Modern Art Exhibition, these paintings by Hu Zhiying have not attracted great attention of the public, and his *Life's Pedigree Picture* even has not got a chance to be shown at a public exhibition. This has something to do with his being in a remote small town in Jiangxi Province and his stubborn and unsociable disposition as well, especially the latter, for the experimental works of ink and wash he produced after he became a postgraduate student of the traditional Chinese painting major at Guangzhou Academy of Fine Arts in 1987 have not attracted due attention of the public either.

Hu Zhiying's artistic concept took shape during his postgraduate student years. It is summed up in the theme of his master's degree thesis *About the Transiency of Art* with the cultural relativism based on liberalism as its core. It is not hard to imagine what might happen to Hu Zhiying against the background of the resurgence of left-deviationist thinking in official ideology in the late 1980s and the early 1990s. He was denied the chance to defend his thesis formally because his thesis does not accord with "Marxism".

Here Hu Zhiying has provided a chance for us to reflect on the turn of art history between the 1980s and the 1990s. The existing writings on the Chinese contemporary art history mostly describe this turn as the degradation of humanistic idealism, and impassive realism (New Generation) under political power, self-consolatory realism (Cynical Realism) and post-modernism characterized by political irony (Political Pop). Such a narrative of art history can also be extended to the post-modernism characterized by cultural irony (Gaudy Art) and the sentimental realism (New Scar Art and Youth Brutal Painting) of the late 1990s as well as the Fashion Realism (New-Cartoon Art) of the early 21st century. In brief, it is a narrative based on realism. Art is understood as an attitude — flattering or ironical — towards the social reality, even those who are against this narrative mostly think from another standpoint also based on realism. For example, some criticize the above mentioned narrative for being cynical or fishing for cheap popularity. They differ in values rather than concept.

However, Hu Zhiying's artistic concept and practice cannot be incorporated into such kind of narrative of art history. Popular images began to be appropriated in his experimental works of ink and wash produced in 1989. For example, a space fighter in the Hollywood film Star Wars appears in his painting Perspective. But Hu Zhiying does not try to express some political attitude or reflect some social reality with them. [2] In this series and his later works, art is not directly related to the social reality. Here the popular images belong only to the world of symbols. They, together with geometrical shapes, Chinese characters, letters, space and "ink and wash" itself, constitute a self-contained body that is fragmented inside. In other words, they are only forms. In this sense, Hu Zhiying is a resolute formalist.

But he is not a formal ornamentalist like Wu Guanzhong. Instead of attaching forms to the conventional pattern of some aesthetical experience, Hu Zhiying emphasizes all along the absoluteness of form; therefore, he has elevated form to the transcendental form in Kantian philosophy. In an article titled The Congenital Comprehensiveness of Ink and Wash Language, he normalizes the creation of ink and wash painting as a comprehensive judgment of congenital "ink and wash language", that is, the "ink and wash language" is elevated to a kind of congenital structure, and specific ink and wash paintings are nothing but the deduction of this congenital structure. [3] Putting aside for the time being the problem of whether Hu Zhiying has properly applied these conceptual categories of Kant, as far as his line of thought in tracing issues of formalism back to Kantian philosophy is concerned, he is undoubtedly profound, for he has taken up the vital part of formalism. Moreover, it has also avoided the cultural conservative line of thought in which "ink and wash" is discussed in terms of cultural identity and has provided a generalized perspective from which the problem of "ink and wash" may be dealt with in an uninhibited way.

This line of thought of his can also be applied to other mediums and genres of art, and it is exactly so in practice. In the painting experiment that began in the early 1990s, he widened the range of the mediums to include materials used in traditional Chinese arts and crafts such as golden powder, silver powder, Chinese lacquer and vermilion. On the other hand, he reduced his "world of symbols". What appears frequently in his series of paintings of the early 1990s are image fragments in the style of landscape paintings of the Song Dynasty. They superimpose on and interweave and contrast with the pictorial and photographical images from Western culture, forming a kind of intricate visual field. Meanwhile, an element of Mannerism has appeared, that is, a given style is enhanced. In these works of Hu Zhiying, it is embodied in the emphasizing of the style of the landscape paintings of the Song Dynasty, especially the display of brushwork itself. Therefore, style is separated from "content" and becomes a kind of pure stylized form. This characteristic has extended to the "Remake Bacon" series Hu Zhiying produce after 2000, leading to a kind of mannered Baconian style.

However, it is impossible that there is no content behind form. Hu Zhiying emphasizes the pure form in order to express — in Lyotard's words — the "inexpressible", something that can also be understood as the above mentioned Paramitality (Jenseitigkeit), Hu Zhiying's key concept. His Ph. D. thesis *On the Paramitality in Literature* of 2002 is a study on the aesthetics of Chinese classical literature based on this term. Though dealing on literature, this thesis suffices to illustrate his artistic concept. In the system of Kantian philosophy, "Jenseitigkeit" (Paramitality) refers to the thing-in-itself beyond man's cognitive ability. For the subject, once attempts are made in aesthetic activity to touch this "Jenseitigkeit" (Paramitality), that is, once attempts are made in cognitive activity to recognize things that cannot be recognized, he will become aware of his limit and then a sense of sublimity will be aroused. Sublimity always belongs to the category of classical aesthetics, yet Lyotard reestablishes the aesthetic value of sublimity in the context of avant-garde. He abstracts "sublimity" from the principle part of Kantian philosophy and thinks that sublimity is the awareness of a certain thing, and that sublimity implies the existence of something inexpressible. [4]

Hu Zhiying's emphasis on "Paramitality" belongs to this sublimity aesthetics. In his practice of painting, this sublimity aesthetics is embodied in two totally different dimensions: on the one hand, he tries to represent some absolute spirituality and break completely the given system of symbols and images and the system of meaning behind it as mere phantoms so as to express the inexpressibility of some spiritual noumenon. On the other hand, he plunges into the thoroughly material level and establishes a kind of opaqueness of meaning with materials (materiality of mediums) and brush strokes (materiality of body) in order to resist the invasion of secular spirit and bear witness to the inexpressibility itself. It is worth mentioning that Lyotard has distinguished these two kinds of sublimity with the former represented by Surrealism and the latter by Abstract Expressionism. In fact, is Hu Zhiying not trying to combine these two together?

Whether Hu Zhiying has reached his goal, and whether his practice for this goal is meaningful, the problem is how "Chinese contemporary art" as we call it should face him and other similar artistic practice and how we should give an account of such a line in our narration of the history of Chinese contemporary art.

Note:

[1] It is interesting that, although many people at that time were influenced by Surrealism, this influence brought about through reading albums of paintings was limited only to visual language. Therefore, Dali's figurative Surrealism, after being stylized, was combined with the theme of cultural reflection of that time and at last formed a manner of Symbolism.

[2] In fact, Political Pop does not express a kind of political attitude; only it is read by the West and then by us as expressing a kind of political attitude.

[3] See Hu Zhiying, *The Congenital Comprehensiveness of Ink and Wash Language*, in *Traditional Chinese Painter*, No. 4, 2000, China Artists Association.

[4] See Lyotard, *The Inhuman*, tr. Luo Guoxiang, Commercial Press, 2000, pp. 131-143.

(Originally published in the *Beyond the Chains of Illusion — Hu Zhiying's Paintings 1989-2009*, China Global Culture Publishing House, 2010)

（图5）生命世系图，1986，布上油彩，170×400cm
(Fig. 5) *Life's Pedigrees Picture*, oil on canvas, 170 × 400 cm

装　置
Installations

胡志颖是"无常"，实际上是要追求一种自由，没有常理，追求一种
更高的境界"道"。"无常"更多的是一种"道"的境界。比放任的
世俗的自由还要高。"无常"是要超越"理"而达到"道"的境界。
——邹跃进

For Hu Zhiying, "transiency" means a pursuit of freedom without any
convention, a pursuit of a higher state, the state of Tao. To a great extent,
"transiency" is a state of Tao, even higher than unrestrained worldly freedom.
"Transiency" means surpassing "reason" and reaching the state of "Tao".
— Zou Yuejin

80年代中期之后的中国美术对欧美现代艺术的吸收与仿效并不是按欧美现代艺术发展轨迹而复述的，而是在"同时性"中效制"历时性"的行动，在这一行动中所展示的样式即是多元同发的……胡志颖的《伪望远镜》分别在多元的探索中为今日中国画坛所瞩目与肯定。

——张　晴

Chinese art after the mid-1980s does not repeat the course of development of European and American modern art when absorbing and imitating modern art of Europe and America. Instead, it takes an action of imitating "diachronic" things in a "synchronic" way, and diversified modes of art are manifested simultaneously in this action....Hu Zhiying's *Pseudo-Telescope*, for its manifold exploration, becomes the focus of public attention and is approved in the painting circles of China today.

— Zhang Qing

伪望远镜，1992，不锈钢，长130cm，直径6.6cm
Pseudo-Telescope, 1992, stainless steel, length 130 cm, diameter 6.6 cm

《伪望远镜》所见之一，1992
View I Seen Through the *Pseudo-Telescope*, 1992

《伪望远镜》所见之二，1992

View II Seen Through the *Pseudo-Telescope*, 1992

《伪望远镜》所见之三，1992
View III Seen Through the *Pseudo-Telescope*, 1992

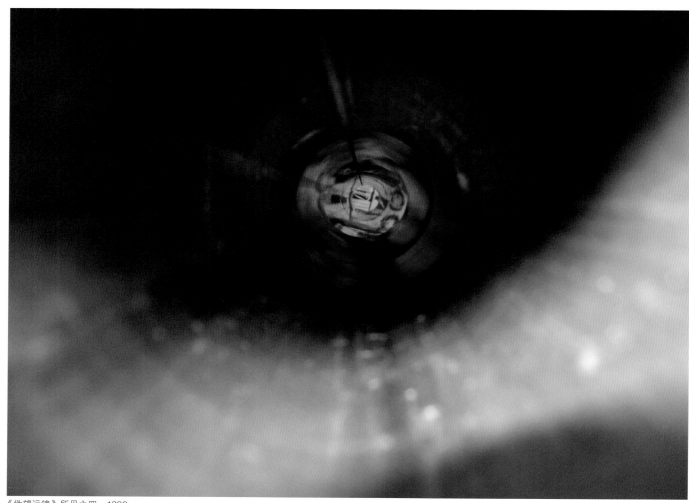

《伪望远镜》所见之四，1992
View IV Seen Through the *Pseudo-Telescope*, 1992

世纪遗恨录之一，2003，综合材料，广州绢麻厂
Century Remorse I, 2003, mixed media, Guangzhou Silk and Linen Factory

世纪遗恨录之二，2003，综合材料，广州绢麻厂
Century Remorse II, 2003, mixed media, Guangzhou Silk and Linen Factory

世纪遗恨录之三，2003，综合材料，广州罐头厂
Century Remorse III, 2003, mixed media, Guangzhou Canning Factory

胡志颖是当代艺术家中卓然不群的一个，他和他的作品只属于艺术，但不属于任何一个艺术群体。
　　　　　　　　　　　　　　　　　　　　　　　　　　　　——张文海

Hu Zhiying is an outstanding contemporary artist. He and his works belong to art only, but not to any art group.
　　　　　　　　　　　　　　　　　　　　　　　　　　　　— Zhang Wenhai

世纪遗恨录之四，2003，综合材料，广州罐头厂
Century Remorse IV, 2003, mixed media, Guangzhou Canning Factory

世纪遗恨录之五，2003，综合材料，广州罐头厂
Century Remorse V, 2003, mixed media, Guangzhou Canning Factory

关于《世纪遗恨录》系列装置

胡志颖

这是一个主体自身——巨型工厂这一庞然大物的遗恨，是一个无法寻找罪恶的无名悔恨，一种孤寂中的自我遗恨。

《世纪遗恨录》的标志就是它为什么一个世纪诞生为那么强大的一个躯体，却在另一个世纪的喧嚣和骚动中孤独地被遗弃。

主体早已迷失自身，似乎一切从来就没有发生，似乎客体由客体而生，孤独地在遗恨中承担着主体的一切而由客体变为主体。也就是说，其中有一种被政治化了的关于客体的"知识"，但不完全是关于客体功能运作的科学；而是对客体力量的驾驭，但又不是征服它的能力；这种知识和这种驾驭构成了某种可以称为客体的"政治技术学"。或许这门"学科"本身就是世界上独一无二的创举。这个客体是被驯化的，可以被驾驭、使用、改造甚至逆转的工具。这种客体被政治驯化为"自动机器"，不仅仅是一种对客体的比喻，而且直接呈现了客体真实地成了政治权力所任意摆布的模型。

这个景象就是无主的遗恨符号本身！在这里，似乎过去没有人出现，现在没有人出现，将来也不会有人出现的"无人区"，是丧失声音的"无声区"，它成了闹市中的"沉寂的极地"！它将历史拉回到五色乱目的现实时空中来做最后的黑白呈现。

它是一个普遍有效的标志性权力之城的遗骸，还是一个世纪遗恨的终极空间？前者通过标志性符号代码和网络而运作，一群人受到另一群人不可逆的支配，导致异化的产生。后者则是主体的内在特性、倾向性最后的栖息地。两种冲突在这个特定的时空中互相消解为宛若空无一物的寂静。

这种孤寂与遗恨相与为一而对周围的一切喧嚣和骚动视若无睹。它从一种君临一切的体验到一种独自遗恨的体验的转变，是在孤寂的状态中反躬自省形成一种极度虚无、脱离正常关系网的世界。这个世界作为一种无声的样态、一种无法加注的行为、一种当下的觉解，揭示了一个怅惘无边、悔恨无已的结构——世纪遗恨。

在这里，遗恨与孤独成为一种被窒息的状态，成为孤独的一面晦暗的镜子和一幅荒寂的景象。当主体的遗恨已深深地淹没在孤独的境域中，一种体验孤寂就构成了主体一切世俗情缘荡然无存的境域。这就使孤寂具备了可以借为主体体验遗恨的内部环境。这种情形就好像遗恨在承认自己的孤独与遗恨有一种亲近关系、相似关系，也好像主体在遗恨之际却让自己用孤独的体验来超度孤独。

它在两个世纪的巨大落差中皈依为寂静的孤独！它把所有的纷繁迷乱消融而凝固为一种恒久不变的沉寂。（图1，2）

2003年于广州绢麻厂（广州绢麻工贸有限公司）

（图1）广州绢麻工贸有限公司大门
(Fig. 1) Gate of Guangzhou Silk and Linen Industry & Trade Co., Ltd.

（图2）广州绢麻工贸有限公司于2008年被拍卖后夷为平地
(Fig. 2) Guangzhou Silk and Linen Industry & Trade Co., Ltd. was leveled to the ground after being auctioned off in 2008

About the Installation Art Series *Century Remorse*

By Hu Zhiying

This is the remorse of the subject itself — a formidable giant, ie., a mammoth factory — an inexplicable remorse for undefinable evil, and a self remorse in solitude.

The indication of *Century Remorse* is why such a big and mighty body which was born in one century should have been abandoned in solitude in another century.

The subject lost itself long ago. It seems that nothing has ever happened and the object originated from itself. In remorse it bears solitarily all that should be borne by the subject and in this process changes from the object to the subject. That is to say, there is in it a kind of politicalized "knowledge" about the object, but it is not entirely a science about the function and mode of operation of the object. It is a control over the power of the object but is not the ability to conquer it. This knowledge and this control constitute what can be called "political technology" of the object. Perhaps this "discipline" is itself a unique undertaking in the world. This object has been tamed. It is a tool that can be controlled, used, transformed or even reversed. That this object has been tamed by politics into an "automatic machine" is not only a figure of speech. It indicates directly that the object has really become a model the political power can manipulate willfully.

This scene is the ownerless sign of remorse itself! It is a "no man's area" where, it seems, no man appeared in the past, appears now, and will appear in the future, and a "silent area" where no sound can be heard. It has become a "silent polar region" in the downtown area of the city! It draws history back into the present dazzling time and space for a last presentation in black and white.

Is it the ruins of a city of universally effective symbolic power or an ultimate space of century remorse? The former operates through symbolic signs, codes and networks and one group of people are dominated irreversibly by another, leading to the emerging of alienation. The latter is the ultimate habitat of the internal characteristics and tendencies of the subject. Their conflict is reduced in this specific time and space to tranquility as if nothing existed.

This solitude and remorse combine into one, and all noises and turmoils around are disregarded. Turning from powerfulness and arrogance to lonely remorse, it became an extremely illusory world breaking away from the normal connections in its meditation in a state of solitude. As a mode of silence, an unexplainable behavior and an instant understanding, this world reveals a structure of infinite anxiety and regret — Century Remorse.

Here remorse and solitude have become a state of being suffocated, a dark mirror of solitude, and a bleak and quiet sight. When the remorse of the subject is submerged deeply in solitude, an experience of solitude will result in the total vanishment of the subject's worldly relations. This makes solitude an inner environment where the subject may experience the remorse. In this case, it seems that remorse admits that its solitude is close and similar to remorse, and that at the time of remorse the subject lets itself release the remorse with its own remorse.

With poignant contrast between its fates in two centuries it is reduced to quiet solitude! It has reduced all complexities and confusions to eternal silence. (Fig. 1, Fig. 2)

2003, Guangzhou Silk and Linen Factory (Guangzhou Silk and Linen Industry & Trade Co., Ltd.)

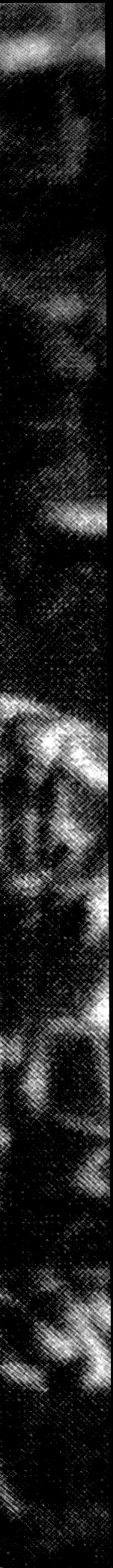

胡志颖的风格和艺术生涯显然没有大部分新潮流中的当代艺术（包括
中国与西方）的特征，而与那些最终留下巨大的历史遗产的大师要接
近得多。

——迪迪埃·赫希

Hu Zhiying's style and career are clearly uncharacteristic of that of most of the
new wave of contemporary art (both Chinese and Western) and much closer
to those who have ended up leaving a huge historical legacy.

— Didier Hirsch

1959 己亥
11月12日生于江西赣州，湖南湘阴人。笔名玉令。

1966 丙午 七岁
随父母从赣南迁至赣东北。文化大革命开始后，武斗残酷。离开父母，转至江西乐平山村随伯父、伯母、堂姐，干农活、上学，前后六年。画毛泽东像、文革英雄人物像，有时画文革内容的漫画组画，张贴于村头。

1972 壬子 十三岁
回到江西上饶父母身边。临摹样板戏《智取威虎山》、《沙家浜》、《红灯记》、《三打白骨精》、《列宁在十月》、《列宁在1918》连环画等。

1973 癸丑 十四岁
此后四年间陆续参加地区、市、县群艺馆、文化馆等机构组织的美术学习班、美术创作学习班。

1974 甲寅 十五岁
读高中时为班级出宣传报，开门办学时为工厂、村庄、部队出宣传报。以中学生开门办学学工、学农、学军为题材学习创作。

1975 乙卯 十六岁
创作新工笔画，入选"江西省少年儿童绘画展览"（南昌）。据王力《诗词格律》，自学格律诗词。

1976 丙辰 十七岁
读完高中后，为县文化馆画宣传画。同时在素描、水粉、油画、国画诸方面做大量实践。

1977 丁巳 十八岁
恢复高考，考入位于南昌市的江西师范学院艺术系美术专业。从江西人民出版社借阅外国画册，其中包括东德（德意志民主共和国）新艺术画册和刊物，极为震惊，并在创作中借鉴其造型、笔触、色彩等因素。

1978 戊午 十九岁
7–8月暑期参加地区群艺馆美术创作学习班。
购得"法国十九世纪农村风景绘画展"（冰封数十年后首次西方名画原作展在上海举行）图录，认真研习，开始注重西欧油画技术，逐渐摆脱前苏联油画技术语言的影响。对《美术丛刊》中介绍西方艺术、特别是现代主义艺术尤为兴奋。

1979 己未 二十岁
8月以鲁迅短篇小说为内容创作《过客》（纸上油彩）。
邮购《外国美术资料选》（浙江美术学院当年创办的内部刊物，后更名为《美术译丛》正式公开发行），《世界美术》等刊物，对其中介绍西方现代主义艺术尤为兴奋，特别喜欢超现实主义，此后深受其影响。
12月创作《受到上帝祝福的幸运的殉道者》（后更名《无辜》，纸上水粉），因展现文革武斗血腥场面，仅在江西师范学院艺术系内部短暂展出。

1980 庚申 二十一岁
写生作品《盆中鱼》（纸上油彩）。
毕业创作《无题》（布上油彩，玻璃碎，沙砾，拼贴）借鉴超现实主义方法表现没有明确主题的历史与现代交织的场景，是学校当时唯一的一幅超现实主义的作品。

1981 辛酉 二十二岁
被分配在江西上饶县中学初中部（位于新开垦的山头），任美术教师。创作巨幅素描《过年》等作品。写生《鸡冠花》、《反光》（纸上油彩）。
赴上海参观"波士顿博物馆藏美国名画原作展"（包括古代及现代两部分），首次观摩西方绘画原作。
自行参加农村义务劳动"双抢"（夏季割稻、种稻）。

1960年一岁和母亲在江西赣州
One-year-old Hu Zhiying and his mother in Ganzhou of Jianxi Province in 1960

1967年在江西乐平农村
In the countryside in Leping of Jianxi Province in 1967

1977年高考前练习素描
Practising drawing before the university entrance examination in 1977

1978年在南昌读大学时参观八大山人书画陈列馆
Visiting the Badashanren Painting and Calligraphy Memorial during his college days in Nanchang in 1978

过客，1979，纸上布上油彩，120×80cm
A Passing Traveler, 1979, oil on paper and canvas, 120 × 80 cm

戴棉帽的青年，1980，纸上木炭，84×60cm
Young Man Wearing a Cotton-Padded-Cap, 1980, charcoal on paper, 84 × 60 cm

鸡冠花，1981，纸上布上油彩，52.8×39.5cm
Cockscombs, 1981, oil on paper and canvas, 52.8 × 39.5 cm

1959

Hu Zhiying, a native of Xiangyin County of Hunan Province with Yu Ling as his penname, was born in Ganzhou of Jiangxi Province in November 12.

1966

Moved from the southern part to the northeastern part of Jiangxi Province with his parents. After the Cultural Revolution began, cruel violent conflicts took place here and there. He had to leave his parents and live together with his uncle, his aunt and his cousin for six years in a mountain village near Leping in Jiangxi Province, where he attended school and did farm work in spare time. He painted the portraits of Mao Zedong and of heroes of the Cultural Revolution, and sometimes series of caricatures the subject of which had something to do with the Cultural Revolution, and put them up on the walls at the village entrance.

1972

Lived with his parents again in Shangrao of Jingxi Province. Copied the pages in picture-story books including those depicting model Peking operas such as *Taking Tiger Mountain by Strategy, Shachiapang, The Red Lantern*, and also *Monkey Subdues White-Skeleton Demon, Lenin in October, Lenin in 1918*, etc.

1973

Attended some art training classes and artistic creation training classes organized by such institutions as prefecture, municipal or county mass art centers or cultural centers during that year and the following three years.

1974

As a senior middle school student, he produced wall newspapers for his grade when at school and for factories, villages or military units during the days of open-door schooling. He learned to produce works of art, with middle school students who were learning industrial production, agricultural production and military affairs in open-door schooling as the subject matter.

1975

Some new meticulous paintings he produced were chosen to be shown at the *Jiangxi Province Children's Paintings Exhibition* (Nanchang).
Taught himself to write poems and Ci with strict tonal patterns and rhyme schemes according to Wang Li's *Metrical Patterns of Poetry*.

1976

After he finished senior middle school, he painted picture posters for the county cultural center. And meanwhile, he practised a lot in drawing, gouache, oil painting and traditional Chinese painting.

1977

After the university entrance examination was resumed, he was admitted to the Fine Arts Programme in the Art Department of Jiangxi Normal College in Nanchang. He was greatly astonished when he glanced over the foreign albums of paintings he had borrowed from Jiangxi People's Publishing House, including new art albums and periodicals from East Germany (German Democratic Republic). He began to draw on foreign elements of form, brushstroke and color in his creation.

1978

In July and August, during the summer vacation, he attended the artistic creation training class organized by the prefecture mass art center.
He bought a copy of the catalogue of *The Exhibition of the 19th Century French Rural Landscape Paintings* (was held in Shanghai, the first exhibition of originals of Western famous paintings held in China in several decades), and studied it carefully. He began to lay stress on the oil painting techniques of Western Europe and gradually got rid of the influence of the oil painting techniques and language of the former Soviet Union. He was especially excited about the accounts of Western art, and modernist art in particular, given in the *Fine Art Series*.

1979

Produced *A Passing Traveler* (oil on paper) in August with a short story by Lu Xun as its subject.
Purchased such periodicals as *Selected Data of Foreign Art* (a periodical for restricted circulation the Zhejiang Academy of Fine Arts began to publish in that year, later published formally and publicly with the new title *Fine Art Translations*) and *World Art* by mail order and was especially excited about the accounts of Western art given in them. He loved surrealism in particular and was influenced profoundly by it thereafter.
Produced *The Fortunate Martyrs Blessed by God* (later entitled *Innocence*, gouache on paper) in December. But this painting was on show only for a short duration within the Art Department of Jiangxi Normal College for it showed a bloody scene of a violent conflict during the Cultural Revolution.

1980

Produced *Fish in the Basin* (oil on paper), a painting from nature .
His graduation work *Untitled* (oil, fragments of glass, grit and collage on canvas), using the technique of surrealism, depicted a scene, without a clear theme, interweaving history with modern times. It was the only surrealistic work at his college at that time.

1981

Assigned to the position of art teacher in the junior section of Shangrao County Middle School (situated on a newly-reclaimed hilltop) in Jiangxi Province. Produced large-scale drawings *Celebrating the New Year*, etc., and paintings from nature *Cockscomb* and *Reflection of Light* (oil on paper).
Went to Shanghai and visited the *Exhibition of Originals of Famous American Paintings from the Collection of Boston Museum* (consisting of two parts, the ancient and the modern), observing the original works of West painting for the first time.
Took part in the voluntary labor of rush-harvesting and rush-sowing in the countryside by himself.

1982 壬戌 二十三岁
　　被调到江西上饶县赣剧团任美工。随剧团下乡演出，写生《草垛》（纸上油彩）。
　　创作《跳神》、《焦大骂街》、《阿Q画押》等国画、水墨作品。
　　创作短篇小说《病》。

1983 癸亥 二十四岁
　　到江西道教名山葛仙山（葛玄道场）写生，作水墨及油画；又到铅山写生。

1984 甲子 二十五岁
　　创作《万世之业》（布上油彩）。
　　赴上海参观"法国鲁佛尔博物馆（卢浮宫）二百五十年藏画展"（从古代到后印象派）。油画技术深受影响。
　　为鲁迅《为了忘却的纪念》作插图。
　　创作意识流小说《中国之九九八十一》。

1985 乙丑 二十六岁
　　被调到江西上饶师范任美术教师。
　　创作《超人》（布上油彩）。

1986 丙寅 二十七岁
　　创作《生命世系图》（布上油彩，后更名《阴阳界》）。

1987 丁卯 二十八岁
　　7月创作《古董》（布上油彩）。
　　8月创作《坐藤椅的肖像》（布上油彩）。
　　9月考入广州美术学院中国画系中国画专业研究生，从尚涛先生学习国画、书法；从广东省文史馆黄文宽先生治国学、金石学。读研究生期间，从广州图书馆、中山图书馆借阅大量哲学、文化以及现代文学类书籍。《研究生三年学习计划》将《艺术无常论》作为毕业论文。

1988 戊辰 二十九岁
　　6月撰写哲学课程论文《无常论》，（实为毕业论文《艺术无常论》之哲学基础），通过。

1989 己巳 三十岁
　　5月至7月旅历中国二十个省、市、自治区，行程四万一千三百余里。
　　创作《大昭寺印象》、《天河》、《透视》、《天风海雨》、《天风海雨（二）》、《阴阳无间》、《热带雨林》、《山水》系列、《正楷》、《草书》等巨幅现代水墨画。
　　导师黄文宽先生不幸逝世。
　　整理十年格律诗词稿，集为《旻堂十年诗词存》。
　　创作多幅抽象表现主义风格的作品《绘画》系列（宣纸上硃砂、墨、油彩、丙烯）。

1990 庚午 三十一岁
　　撰写毕业论文《艺术无常论》。
　　研究生毕业展展出《山水》系列、巨幅水墨图片及书法对联。
　　毕业论文《艺术无常论》（依学习计划完成）被广州美术学院理论教研室主任迟轲扣以政治帽子而遭否定，未举行答辩，未获毕业证和硕士学位证。当时广州美术学院青年教师（包括理论教研室教师）、已毕业研究生、在校研究生联名向学院以及上级主管部门反映，表示应尊重学术自由，不应将学术和行政相混淆。（2001年天津美术学院《北方美术》全文刊载《艺术无常论》。中国人民大学报刊资料中心将此文编入2001年《造型艺术理论索引》。）
　　9月份后，继续留广州美术学院，在向广东省高教厅等上级主管部门反映，未果。
　　以1989年全国考察收集的材料，以及由此而思考的问题为基础，撰写《中国美术考察报告》。
　　创作《自画像》（布上油彩、蛋胶）。创作巨幅抽象表现主义风格的作品《绘画14号》（板上油彩、油漆），后广州美术学院研究生宿舍拆迁时被毁，现仅存小草稿。
　　11月应李正天先生之邀，组织、操办全国征稿和约稿的"中国当代书法展"（在广州、北京展出）。
　　设计行为艺术《聊天》（计划在展厅内表演）。

超人，1985，布上油彩，170×86cm
Superwoman, 1985, oil on canvas, 170 × 86 cm

1989年在广州美院读研究生
At Guangzhou Academy of Fine Arts as a postgraduate student in 1989

广州美术学院1990届研究生毕业作品展
Graduation Works Exhibition of Postgraduates of 1990 at the Guangzhou Academy of Arts

1990年在广州美术学院接受法国记者采访
Being interviewed by a French reporter at Guangzhou Academy of Fine Arts in 1990

1982

Transferred to the Shangrao County Jiangxi Opera Troupe in Jiangxi Province, where he worked as an art designer. During the period when the troupe was giving performances in the countryside, he produced *Haystack* (oil on paper, painting from nature) there.

Produced traditional Chinese paintings and ink and wash paintings *Sorcerer's Dance in a Trance*, *Jiao Da Shouting Abuse in Public*, *Ah Q Making His Cross*, etc.

Wrote the short story *Illness*.

1983

Went to paint from nature in the Gexian Mountains (Ge Xuan's site of performing Taoist rites), produced ink and wash paintings and oil paintings, and went to paint from nature in the Qianshan Mountains.

1984

Produced *An Undertaking for All Ages* (oil on canvas).

Went to Shanghai and visited the *250-Year Collection of Louvre in French* (from ancient times to post-impressionism). His oil painting techniques were profoundly influenced.

Made illustrations for Lu Xun's *Commemoration for the Sake of Oblivion*.

Wrote the story *China, Nine Times Nine is Eighty-One* using the technique of stream of consciousness.

1985

Transferred to the position of art teacher at Shangrao Normal College in Jiangxi Province.

Produced *Superwoman* (oil on canvas).

1986

Produced *Life's Pedigrees Picture* (oil on canvas, later changed with the new title This World and Nether World).

1987

Produced *Antiques* (oil on canvas) in July .

Produced *Portrait of a ure on a Cane Chair* (oil on canvas) in August.

Admitted to the Traditional Chinese Painting Department of Guangzhou Academy of Fine Arts as a postgraduate student in September, majoring in Chinese Traditional Painting. Studied traditional Chinese painting and calligraphy under Mr. Shang Tao and Chinese culture and epigraphy under Mr. Huang Wenkuan of Guangdong Province Research Institute of Culture and History. As a postgraduate student, he read a large number of books of philosophy, culture and modern literature borrowed from Guangzhou Library and Sun Yat-sen Library. In his *Study Plan for the Three Postgraduate Years*, he listed *About the Transiency of Art* as his graduation thesis.

1988

Wrote the thesis for philosophy course in June titled *About Transiency* (in fact the philosophical foundation of his graduation thesis *About the Transiency of Art*) and this thesis was approved.

1989

Traveled in 20 provinces, municipalities and autonomous regions in China from May to July, covering more than twenty thousand and six hundred kilometer.

Produced huge modern ink and wash paintings including The Impression of *Zuglakang Monastery*, *Galaxy*, *Perspective, Nature's Mystery, Nature's Mystery (2)*, *Yin and Yang Close to Each Other*, *Tropical Rain Forest*, *Mountains and Waters* series, *Regular Script* and *Cursive Hand*.

Mr. Huang Wenkuan, his tutor, passed away.

Sorted out his poems and Ci poems with strict tonal patterns and rhyme schemes written in the past ten years and compiled them into a volume titled *Min Tang Poetry of a Decade*.

Produced a number of works in the style of abstract expressionism in the *Painting* series (cinnabar, ink, oil and acrylic on rice paper).

1990

Wrote his graduation thesis *About the Transiency of Art*.

His *Mountains and Waters* series, huge pictures of ink and wash and an antithetical couplet as a work of calligraphy were on show at the graduation works exhibition.

His graduation thesis *About the Transiency of Art* (completed according to his plan of study) was negated by Chi Ke, director of the Theory Teaching and Research Section of Guangzhou Academy of Fine Arts, who put a political label on it. He was denied the chance to defend his thesis and eventually fail to acquire the diploma and the master's degree certificate. At that time, young teachers (including those of the Theory Teaching and Research Section), postgraduates who had finished their programme and those who were still studying at Guangzhou Academy of Fine Arts jointly expressed their opinion to the Academy authorities and authorities at a higher level responsible for the work concerned that academic freedom should be respected and learning should not be confused with administration. (The full text of *About the Transiency of Art* was published in *Northern Art*, journal of Tianjin Academy of Fine Arts in 2001. The title of his thesis was included in the *Index of Theory of Plastic Art* of 2001 by Center of Data from Newspapers and Magazines of Renmin University of China.)

Still stayed at Guangzhou Academy of Fine Arts after September. He reported this matter to Department of Higher Education of Guangdong Province and other authorities at a higher level responsible for the work concerned with the hope that it would be properly resolved, but in vain.

Wrote "Report on an Investigation of Chinese Art" on the basis of the materials collected during the nationwide investigation in 1989 and his consideration about them.

Produced *Self-Portrait* (oil and tempera on canvas) and the huge painting in the style of abstract expressionism *Painting No. 14* (oil and paint on panel). The latter was destroyed later when the dormitories of postgraduate students of Guangzhou Academy of Fine Arts were pull down and students resettled, and only the small rough sketch of it survived.

In November, invited by Mr. Li Zhengtian to organize and arrange *China Contemporary Calligraphy Exhibition* (held in Guangzhou and Beijing) for which works were solicited and invited throughout the country.

Designed the performance *Chatting* (he originally planned to put it on in the exhibition hall).

1991 辛未 三十二岁

创作《红白黑》（现成品、拼贴）。在广州艺术家画廊展览。
创作《拼贴》（现成品、拼贴，已毁）。
创作《文字改革》（书写、拼贴、丝网印刷）。
9月份，离开广州美术学院，被分配到广州市工艺美术职业中学工作。
创作《眼对眼，仿彼得》、《浪子与火》（布上油彩）。
开始陆续收集资料，准备编撰《西方当代艺术状态》。

1992 壬申 三十三岁

绘画风格发生巨变。采用叠影的方式综合东西不同文化元素，并以油彩、金粉、银粉、大漆、硍砞、水墨等综合材料，创作《文字》系列作品。
参加“大尾象・联合艺术展”（广东广播电视大学大楼），展出绘画作品《文字》系列和装置作品《伪望远镜》。

1993 癸酉 三十四岁

撰写《德国当代画家阿尔贝特・厄伦》。

1994 甲戌 三十五岁

与画家黄少垠结褵上川岛。
创作《数学》系列（综合材料）。
撰写《德国当代艺术理论家克劳斯・霍内夫》。
在广州华南植物园实施行为艺术《聊天》（原计划在展厅内）。

1995 乙亥 三十六岁

女儿出生。
创作《天文》系列（综合材料）。
路德维希博物馆派专家前来选购藏品。四幅作品被收藏。
调入华南师范大学美术系工作。受国家教委之聘，参与编撰全国统编高校教材《中国美术史及作品鉴赏》。
创作中篇小说《纪年表》。

1996 丙子 三十七岁

6月，作品《文字》、《数学》、《天文》系列参加由德国艺术研究机构主办的“China-Aktuelles aus 15 Ateliers”（15位中国当代艺术家工作室）在德国慕尼黑展出。
10月，作品《文字》、《数学》、《天文》系列参加瑞士“李特曼文化计划”——“CHINA NOW！”（今日中国！）在巴塞尔展览。
创作作品《黄金含量中》，并以传真形式参加“上海首届国际传真艺术展”。
参加中国当代艺术展览——“PLATFORM I”在荷兰阿姆斯特丹展出。
《山水》系列作品，由德国路德维希博物馆收藏。
创作《方程式》系列（综合材料）。

1997 丁丑 三十八岁

创作《原子》系列（综合材料）。
创作《内典录》系列（水墨、丙烯、木炭）。
参加中国当代艺术展览——“CHINA NOW！”（今日中国！）在日本东京、大阪等五个城市展出。

1992年大尾象・联合艺术展
Big-Tail Elephant, United Art Exhibition in 1992

1991年广州艺术家画廊展览
Exhibition at Guangzhou Artists Gallery in 1991

1992年胡志颖和黄少垠在广州
Hu Zhiying and Huang Shaoyin in Guangzhou in 1992

1992年大尾象・联合艺术展（胡志颖、林一林、梁钜辉、陈劭雄和徐坦）
Big-Tail Elephant, Unite Art Exhibition in 1992 (Hu Zhiying, Lin Yilin, Liang Juhui, Chen Shaoxiong and Xu Tan)

1992年大尾象・联合艺术展展览研讨会
Symposium on *Big-Tail Elephant, United Art Exhibition* in 1992

1995年路德维希博物馆购买藏品
The experts from Ludwig Museum buying his works in 1995

1996年瑞士展览 "今日中国！"
The exhibition *CHINA NOW!* in Switzerland in 1996

1996年德国展览 "15位中国当代艺术家工作室"（1）
The exhibition *China-Aktuelles aus 15 Ateliers* in Germany in 1996 (1)

1991

Produced *Red, White and Black* (readymade and collage), which was exhibited at Guangzhou Artists Gallery.

Produced *Collage* (readymade and collage, destroyed).

Produced *Reform of a Writing System* (writing, collage and screen printing).

Left Guangzhou Academy of Fine Arts in September and assigned to Guangzhou Arts and Crafts Vocational Secondary School.

Produced *Eye to Eye, After Peter* and *Prodigal Son and Fire* (oil on canvas).

Began to collect data for his book *The State of Western Contemporary Art*.

1992

His style of painting changed greatly. Synthesizing different cultural elements of the East and the West and using mixed media including oil, golden powder, silver powder, lacquer, vermilion, ink and wash, he produced the *Characters* series in the layered manner.

Participated in the *Big-Tail Elephant, United Art Exhibition* (Building of Guangdong Radio and Television University), and his paintings of the *Characters* series and the installation *Pseudo Telescope* were on show.

1993

Wrote the *German Contemporary Artist Albert Oehlen*.

1994

The wedding ceremony of Hu Zhiying and the painter Huang Shaoyin was held on the Shangchuan Islands.

Produced the *Mathematics* series (mixed media).

Wrote *Klaus Honnef: Contemporary Art Theorist in Germany*.

The performance *Chatting* was put on in South China Botanical Garden of Guangzhou (he originally planned to put it on in the exhibition hall).

1995

His daughter was born.

Produced the *Astronomy* series (mixed media).

An expert was dispatched by Ludwig Museum to choose his works; four of his works were collected.

Transferred to work in the Fine Art Department of South China Normal University. Invited by the State Education Commission, he participated in the compilation of *History of Chinese Fine Arts and Appreciation of Works of Art*, a national university textbook compiled for general use.

Produced the medium-length novel titled *THE ANNALS*.

1996

In June, his works *Characters*, *Mathematics* and *Astronomy* series were on show at *China-Aktuelles aus 15 Ateliers* sponsored by German art research institutions and held in Munich of Germany.

In October, his works *Characters*, *Mathematics*, *Astronomy* series were exhibited in Basel at the *China Now* exhibition of the Litman Culture Project of Switzerland.

Produced *Medium Gold Content*, which was on show in the form of a fax at the 1st Shanghai International Fax Art Exhibition.

Participated in the Chinese contemporary art exhibition *PLATFORM 1* held in Amsterdam, Netherlands.

His paintings of the *Mountains and Waters* series were collected by Ludwig Museum, Cologne.

Produced his *Equation* series (mixed media).

1997

Produced his *Atoms* series (mixed media).

Produced his *Buddhist Scriptures* series (ink, wash, acrylic and charcoal).

Participated in *CHINA NOW!*, an exhibition of Chinese contemporary art held in five cities of Japan including Tokyo and Osaka.

1996年德国展览 "15位中国当代艺术家工作室"（2）
The exhibition *China-Aktuelles aus 15 Ateliers* in Germany in 1996 (2)

1996年荷兰展览 "PLATFORM 1"
The exhibition *PLATFORM 1* in the Netherlands in 1996

1998 戊寅 三十九岁
晋升副教授。
创作《内典录》（水墨、丙烯、木炭）系列。
撰写《水墨语言的先天综合性》。
创作中篇小说《纪年表》在投稿过程中遗失，根据不完整草稿重写。
"CHINA NOW！"（今日中国！）继续在日本东京、大阪等五个城市展出。

1999 己卯 四十岁
创作《内典录》系列。
撰写《发现的逻辑——中国当代艺术批评家与艺术家互动透视》。
9月考入暨南大学中文系，攻读文艺学专业博士学位，师从蒋述卓先生。
撰写博士学位论文《文学彼岸性研究》纲要。
撰写《技术原则——油画教学启示录》。
油画《古董》和系列水墨画《内典录》，在法国国家电视二台专题节目"1999年广州跨文化艺术节"（由国际知名制片人罗伯特·卡恩 [Robert Cahen] 制作）中介绍，巴黎。

2000 庚辰 四十一岁
撰写博士学位论文《文学彼岸性研究》第一、二部分。
翻译英国剧作家保尔·艾布莱曼剧本《实验》（包家仁校），并撰写《"形式"的逻辑——评艾布莱曼剧本〈实验〉》。

2001 辛巳 四十二岁
撰写博士学位论文《文学彼岸性研究》第三、四部分。
举办"胡志颖作品展"，中央美术学院美术馆。

2002 壬午 四十三岁
对《文学彼岸性研究》反复易稿，三年大部分时间都用于撰写博士学位论文《文学彼岸性研究》。
6月，博士学位论文答辩时，因选题和方法论而引起争议，答辩过程长达两个多小时。通过答辩并获得博士学位。
在多年收集积累资料的基础上，编撰《西方当代艺术状态》。

2003 癸未 四十四岁
修改《文学彼岸性研究》，并补充"从宇宙观照到人生彻悟"部分。
专著《文学彼岸性研究》由中国社会科学出版社出版；编著《西方当代艺术状态》（李本正校）由人民美术出版社出版。
胡志颖作品展，广东美术馆。
以废弃的国营大厂广州绢麻厂为环境，制作系列装置《世纪遗恨录》。
继续创作未完成的《内典录》系列（丙烯，墨，木炭，油画棒，植物颜料）。

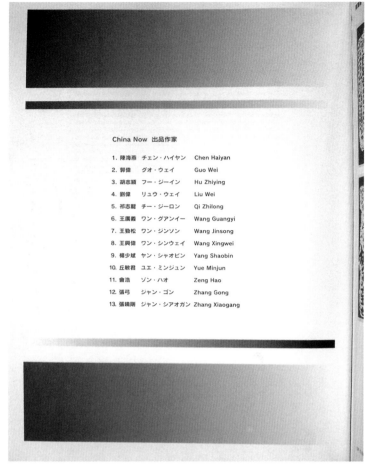

1998年日本展览（1）
Exhibition in Japan in 1998 (1)

China Now 出品作家

1. 陈海燕	チェン・ハイヤン	Chen Haiyan
2. 郭伟	グオ・ウェイ	Guo Wei
3. 胡志颖	フー・ジーイン	Hu Zhiying
4. 刘伟	リュウ・ウェイ	Liu Wei
5. 祁志龙	チー・ジーロン	Qi Zhilong
6. 王广义	ワン・グアンイー	Wang Guangyi
7. 王劲松	ワン・ジンソン	Wang Jinsong
8. 王兴伟	ワン・シンウェイ	Wang Xingwei
9. 杨少斌	ヤン・シャオビン	Yang Shaobin
10. 丘敏君	ユエ・ミンジュン	Yue Minjun
11. 曾浩	ゾン・ハオ	Zeng Hao
12. 张弓	ジャン・ゴン	Zhang Gong
13. 张晓刚	ジャン・シアオガン	Zhang Xiaogang

1998年日本展览（2）
Exhibition in Japan in 1998 (2)

1999年广州高校教师艺术展
Guangzhou College and University Teachers Art Exhibition in 1999

1999年法国驻广州总领事馆文化专员马海先生参观工作室
Mr. Christain Merer, Cultural Counselor of the Consulate General of France in Guangzhou, visiting his studio in 1999

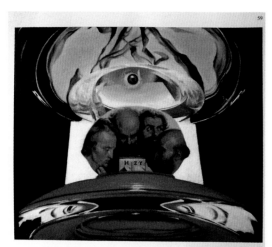

2000年出版的《中国当代高等美术院校实力派教师油画教学对话》，美术高校教材（油画）（1）

Dialogue on Teaching of Oil Painting by Prominent Teachers of Contemporary Art Academies in China published in 2000, a textbook (oil painting) for art academies (1)

2000年出版的《中国当代高等美术院校实力派教师油画教学对话》，美术高校教材（油画）（2）

Dialogue on Teaching of Oil Painting by Prominent Teachers of Contemporary Art Academies in China published in 2000, a textbook (oil painting) for art academies (2)

2001年胡志颖作品展，中央美术学院美术馆

Art Exhibition of Hu Zhiying at Art Gallery of Central Academy of Fine Arts in Beijing in 2001

1998

Promoted to associate professor.

Produced *Buddhist Scriptures* series (ink, wash, acrylic and charcoal).

Wrote *The Congenital Comprehensiveness of Ink and Wash Language*.

The manuscript of his medium-length novel *THE ANNALS* was lost in the process of posting and he had to write it again according to the incomplete draft.

CHINA NOW! continued to be held in five cities of Japan including Tokyo and Osaka.

1999

Produced *Buddhist Scriptures* series.

Wrote *The Logic of Discovery — On the Interaction Between Chinese Contemporary Art Critics and Artists*.

In September, admitted to the Department of Chinese Language of Jinan University, where he studied for a doctor's degree in the programme of the study of art and literature under Mr. Jiang Shuzhuo.

Wrote the outline for his Ph. D. thesis *On the Paramitality in Literature*.

Wrote *Principle of Techniques — Revelations of Oil Painting Teaching*.

His oil painting *Antique* and ink and wash painting series *Buddhist Scriptures* were introduced by the world famous producer Robert Cahen in Paris on French National TV 2 in the special program *Transculturelles in Canton '1999*.

2000

Wrote the first and second part of his Ph. D. thesis *On the Paramitality in Literature*.

Translated the playlet *TESTS* by the English playwright Paul Ableman (and the traslation was revised by Bao Jiaren), and wrote *Logic of "Forms": A Comment on Paul Ableman's Playlet TESTS*.

2001

Wrote the third and fourth part of his Ph. D. thesis *On the Paramitality in Literature*.

Held *Art Exhibition of Hu Zhiying* at the Art Gallery of Central Academy of Fine Arts, Beijing.

2002

Revised his *On the Paramitality in Literature* repeatedly and spent most of the three years in writing this Ph. D. thesis.

In June, in the process of his Ph. D. thesis defence, a debate occurred due to the chosen subject of the thesis and the methodology used. The defence lasted over two hours. At last he succeeded in the defence and got the doctor's degree.

Compiled *The State of Western Contemporary Art* on the basis of the data he had collected and accumulated for many years.

2003

Revised his *On the Paramitality in Literature* and added the part "From Contemplation about the Universe to Thorough Understanding of Life".

His monograph *On the Paramitality in Literature* was published by China Social Sciences Press and *The State of Western Contemporary Art* he compiled (revised by Li Benzheng) was published by People's Fine Arts Publishing House.

Art Exhibition of Hu Zhiying was held at Guangdong Museum of Art.

Produced the installation series *Century Remorse* with an abandoned state-run large factory, the Guangzhou Silk and Linen Factory, as its environment.

Continued to produce the *Buddhist Scriptures* series (acrylic, ink, charcoal, oil crayon and plant pigment).

全家福（在华南植物园）

Photograph of his whole family (in South China Botanical Garden)

2004 甲申 四十五岁
晋升教授。
创作《河山》（布上油彩）。
画风再度发生巨变，借鉴英国画家弗朗西斯·培根的造型，进行再创造，
创作《日历》、《重造培根——蝙蝠与玫瑰》（布上油彩、大漆、丙烯）
系列。
举办"胡志颖艺术展"，江苏美术馆。
撰写《〈"西方后现代艺术流派书系"总序〉错误举要》。

2005 乙酉 四十六岁
创作《重造培根——山君与艳星》（布上油彩、大漆、丙烯）系列。
创作《重造培根——女子角斗》（布上油彩、大漆、丙烯）系列。
创作《重造培根——修女与狒狒》（布上油彩、大漆、丙烯）系列。
举办"胡志颖绘画作品展"，上海大学美术学院。

2006 丙戌 四十七岁
举办"胡志颖作品展"，清华大学美术学院。
创作《重造培根——猫头鹰与灵长类》（布上油彩、大漆、丙烯）系列。
设计装置作品《创世纪——黑冰–白冰》（计划）。
应邀参加"中国名家书画展"，暨南大学博物馆。

2007 丁亥 四十八岁
创作《培根梦与性爱》（布上油彩、大漆、丙烯）系列。
整理自由诗诗稿，集为《碎片》。

2008 戊子 四十九岁
作品应邀赴意大利Piziarte画廊展览。
创作《山河》（布上油彩）。
创作《性爱与文明》（布上油彩、大漆、丙烯）系列。
加入中国美术家协会。

2004年胡志颖艺术展，江苏美术馆
Art Exhibition of Hu Zhiying in Jiangsu Provincial Art Museum in 2004

河山，2004–2005，布上油彩，25.5×20.5cm
Rivers and Mountains, 2004-2005, oil on canvas, 25.5 × 20.5 cm

2005年胡志颖绘画作品展，上海大学美术学院
Paintings Exhibition of Hu Zhiying at at Fine Art College Shanghai University in 2005

2006年胡志颖作品展，清华大学美术学院
Art Exhibition of Hu Zhiying at Academy of Arts & Design of Tsinghua University in Beijing in 2006

工作室
Hu Zhiying's studio

Chinese Painter Hu Zhiying Makes His Bones With Bacon

Down through art history it has been a common practice for artists to pay tribute to other artists by either deliberately adopting aspects of each others' style or copying their works outright (Manet once borrowed an entire composition from Raphael and we're all familiar with Picasso's homages to Rubens and Velazquez.)

In China, where traditional ink painters learn the conventions for depicting various elements of nature by copying the examples in an instruction primer called The Mustard Seed Manual, to copy another artist's work is to confer on him or her the highest kind of honor. In the West, however, the advent of the Appropriation Movement (artists making exact duplicates of works by other artists and blatantly exhibiting them as their own) caused considerable controversy in the 1980s.

All of which brings us to the case of Hu Zhiying, a distinguished contemporary Chinese painter whose powerful series "Remake Bacon," is on view in his exhibition at World Fine Art Gallery, 511 West 25th Street, from January 2 through 31, 2009. (Reception: January 8, 6 to 8p.m.)

The exhibition also includes large mixed media paintings titled "Astronomy" and "Characters," in which, working in a layered postmodern manner akin to David Salle, Zhiying superimposes delicate, linear images of tree limbs and rocks apparently copied in white paint from The Mustard Seed Manual over large semi-abstract landscapes painted in the Western manner. Like ghostly palimpsests, these vestiges of traditional Chinese ink painting seem to comment wryly on issues of influence, copying, and the difference between how originality is viewed in the East and the West. And in doing so, they prime one's mind for this immensely gifted Chinese painter's highly original take on the work of the famous British painter Francis Bacon.

It should be news to no one familiar with his work that Bacon himself was a great copier, not only of Eadweard Muybridge's motion photographs of naked wrestlers, but of earlier painters as well. His paintings of screaming popes, after all, derived directly from postcards of Velazquez's famous portrait "Pope Innocent X" that Bacon copied, subjecting the image to grotesque distortions, transforming a flattering clerical likeness into an image of demonic monster.

Armed with this information, one can now look at Hu Zhiying's "remakes" of another painting by Bacon that the British artist based on one of Muybridge's photograph's of naked wrestlers (placing them on a bed to make the image more sexually suggestive) with a less judgmental eye. And in doing so, one may realize that Zhiying actually transforms the original image even more than Bacon did, making both of the figures blue rather than flesh colored and making one of them appear decidedly feminine (despite the vigorous expressionist strokes that render both semi-abstract.) But the biggest change of all is the huge image of a beautiful woman, cropped at the top of the head and below the breasts, hovering behind the two merged bodies. Painted more realistically, albeit more faintly, she suggests the phantom memory of an erotic encounter, a haunting vision of love long gone. In context, this image is strikingly incongruous, since female figures appear only rarely in Bacon's oeuvre, and are never beautiful like this one.

In the exhibition, this painting is bracketed between two other large canvases to form a triptych, a configuration that Bacon himself often favored. However, while the other two canvases also partake of a Baconesque visual vocabulary of forms, their specific sources are not as readily discernible. For Hu Zhiying has subjected the figures in both can vases to considerably more imagistic deconstruction than Bacon usually did, creating a composition that, in fact, appears to reference certain aspects of Julian Schnabel's abstractions even while retaining the overall compositional thrust and mood of Bacon.

Thus, through his own painterly articulation, Zhiying gives us an interesting insight as to how Bacon influenced Schnabel in terms of form, drama, and showmanship, if not in subject matter. But his own transmutations of the British painter's imagery are even more interesting for their brilliant fluidity, with the central figuratively abusive forms metamorphosing muscularly into sinuous biomorphic clusters set against expanses of fiery red seemingly Abstract Expressionist brushwork from which the tortured Baconish faces emerge when one steps back from the canvas.

In this stately triptych, Zhiying pays tribute to Bacon while creating something new and quite sensational, just as he does in another imaginatively abstracted "remake" of "Painting 1946," the seminal picture juxtaposing sides of beef with a sinister mortician-like figure half-hidden under a black umbrella with which Bacon made his early reputation (itself an amalgam of Soutine's bloody Expressionist carcasses and the Renaissance master Masaccio's fresco of the Trinity.)

With this exhibition at World Fine Art Gallery, Hu Zhiying, who lives in Guangzhou, China, and teaches at the College of Fine Arts of South China Normal University, makes a major statement about the multicultural currents of cross-fertilization of influence, inspiration and innovation that unite painters of the past, present, and future. With Beijing fast becoming one of the major contemporary art capitals of the world, it seems only a matter of time before he makes his bones as an international art star.

—Ed McCormack

Nov./Dec. 2008–Jan. 2009   *GALLERY&STUDIO 31*

2009年纽约《画廊与工作室》
Gallery & Studio (New York, 2009)

2009年应邀赴纽约展览，与经纪人和艺术家在一起。
With brokers and artists when his exhibition was held on invitation in New York in 2009

2009年纽约《画廊指南》
Gallery Guide (New York, 2009)

2004
Promoted to professor.
Produced *Rivers and Mountains* (oil on canvas).
His style greatly changed again, and he produced the *Calendar* and the *Remake Bacon — Bat and Rose series* (oil, lacquer and acrylic on canvas) using the forms of the British painter Francis Bacon as reference.
Art Exhibition of Hu Zhiying was held at Jiangsu Provincial Art Museum, Nanjing.
Wrote *Essentials of the Errors in "Western Post-Modern Art Schools Series"*.

2005
Produced *Remake Bacon — Tiger and Star* series (oil, lacquer and acrylic on canvas).
Produced *Remake Bacon — Female Wrestling* series (oil, lacquer and acrylic on canvas).
Produced *Remake Bacon — Nun and Baboon* series (oil, lacquer and acrylic on canvas).
Paintings Exhibition of Hu Zhiying was held at Fine Art College of Shanghai University, Shanghai.

2006
Exhibition of Works by Hu Zhiying was held at the Academy of Fine Arts in Tsing Hua University, Beijing.
Produced *Remake Bacon — Owl and Primates* series (oil, lacquer and acrylic on canvas).
Designed the installation *Genesis — Black Ice-White Ice* (plan).
Participated in the Painting and Calligraphy Exhibition of Accomplished Masters in China on invitation at the Museum of Jinan University, Guangzhou.

2007
Produced *Bacon's Dream and Sex* series (oil, lacquer and acrylic on canvas).
Sorted out his free verses and compiled them into his *Fragments*.

2008
His works were exhibited at the Galleria Piziarte in Italy on invitation.
Produced *Mountains and Rivers* (oil on canvas).
Produced *Sex and Civilization* series (oil, lacquer and acrylic on canvas).
Joined the Chinese Artists Association.

山河，2008~2011，布上油彩，210 × 170cm
Mountains and Rivers, 2008-2011, oil on canvas, 210 × 170 cm

2009年《纽约艺术杂志》
NY Arts Magazine (New York, 2009)

2009 己丑 五十岁
　　1月应邀赴美国纽约国际美术馆（WORLD FINE ART INC.）举办展览。纽约《画廊指南》、《画廊与工作室》报道并刊载作品。《美国艺术》作新闻报道。
　　创作《红灯区》（布上油彩、大漆、丙烯）系列作品。
　　创作《伸出你的舌头空荡荡》（布上丙烯、大漆）系列作品。
　　创作《玫瑰之名》（布上丙烯、油彩、大漆）系列作品。
　　7月在北京789艺术区K艺术空间举办"无常与放任——胡志颖·黄少垠绘画展"。

2010 庚寅 五十一岁
　　2月参加纽约写实主义画廊（REALISM GALERRY）举办的群展"季节与色彩"。展览消息及作品载《画廊与工作室》、《纽约艺术杂志》、《纽约国际艺术博览会报》等专业刊物。
　　3月在华南植物园创作装置《无主的锤子》。
　　创作《三位一体——仙花，神女，圣徒》（布上油彩、大漆、丙烯）系列作品。
　　创作《白月》（布上油彩、大漆、丙烯）系列作品。
　　6月—7月北京墙美术馆主办二十年作品回顾展《在幻象锁链的彼岸——胡志颖绘画作品1989–2009》，并出版作品集。
　　获德国莱比锡"2010国际棕榈艺术奖"之"成就奖"。

2011 辛卯 五十二岁
　　画册《胡志颖作品集》由海风出版社出版。

2009年"无常与放任 —— 胡志颖·黄少垠绘画展"展览现场（杨卫、高岭、邹跃进、贾方舟、胡志颖、黄少垠、鲍栋、吴鸿）
Scene of the exhibition *Transiency and Indulge — Hu Zhiying & Huang Shaoyin Drawing* in 2009 (Yang Wei, Gao Ling, Zou Yuejin, Jia Fangzhou, Hu Zhiying, Huang Shaoyin, Bao Dong, and Wu Hong)

2009年美国独立批评家、策展人罗宾参观胡志颖作品
American independent critic and curator Robin visiting Hu Zhiying's works in 2009

2009年爱尔兰裔法国收藏家参观胡志颖作品
France collectors of Ireland descent visiting Hu Zhiying's works in 2009

2009年"无常与放任——胡志颖·黄少垠绘画展"座谈会在艺术国际（高岭、贾方舟、鲍栋、吴鸿、黄少垠、胡志颖、杨卫、邹跃进）
2009 Forum on the *Transiency and Indulge — Hu Zhiying & Huang Shaoyin Drawing* at Art Artintern.net (Gao Ling, Jia Fangzhou, Bao Dong, Wu Hong, Huang Shaoyin, Hu Zhiying, Yang Wei, and Zou Yuejin)

《东方艺术·大家》封面（2010）
Cover of *Oriental Art-Master* (2010)

和策展人鲍栋在2010年20年回顾展《在幻想锁链的彼岸——胡志颖绘画作品1989~2009》
With curator Bao Dong at the retrospective exhibition of his works in the past twenty years *Beyond the Chains of Illusion — Hu Zhiying's Paintings 1989-2009* in 2010

2010年20年回顾展《在幻想锁链的彼岸——胡志颖绘画作品1989~2009》媒体采访
Bing interviewed by the media at the retrospective exhibition of his works in the past twenty years *Beyond the Chains of Illusion — Hu Zhiying's Paintings 1989-2009* in 2010

胡志颖、高名潞
Hu Zhiying and Gao Minglu

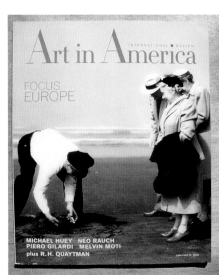

《美国艺术》（2010，No.6）
Art in America (No.6, 2010)

王璜生、胡志颖
Wang Huangsheng and Hu Zhiying

2009

In January, held an exhibition in the New York World Fine Art Inc. in America on invitation. Reports about the exhibition and some of his works were published in *Gallery Guide* and *Gallery & Studio*, periodicals in New York. News report about this exhibition was given in *Art in America*.

Produced the *Red-Light District* series (oil, lacquer and acrylic on canvas).

Produced the *Out Your Empty Tongue* series (oil, Lacquer and acrylic on canvas).

Produced The *Name of the Rose* series (oil, Lacquer and acrylic on canvas).

In July, held the *Transiency and Indulgence — Hu Zhiying and Huang Shaoyin's Drawing* at the K Art Space in 798 Art District, Beijing.

2010

Participated in the group exhibition *Season and Color* held by the Realism Gallery of New York in February. News about this exhibition and some of his works were published in professional periodicals including *Gallery & Studio*, *NY Arts Magazine* and *Art Fairs International News Paper* (New York).

Produced the installation *Ownerless Hammer* in South China Botanical Garden of Guangzhou in March.

Produced the *Trinity — Fairy Flower, Goddess and Saint* series (oil, Lacquer and acrylic on canvas).

Produced the *White Moon* series (oil, Lacquer and acrylic on canvas).

Held *Beyond the Chains of Illusion — Hu Zhiying's Paintings 1989-2009*, a retrospective exhibition of his works in the past twenty years, at the Wall Art Museum of Beijing from June to July, and published a collection of his works.

Won the *Merit Award* of the *International Palm Art Award 2010*, Leipzig, Germany.

2011

A Collection of Works by Hu Zhiying was published by Haifeng Publishing House.

批评家、策展人、收藏家、经纪人简介（以本书出现先后为序）：

A Brief Introduction to Critics, Curators, Collectors and Dealers (in order of appearance in the album) :

高名潞：批评家，策展人，"意派"理论创立者。哈佛大学博士，美国匹兹堡大学艺术和建筑史系研究教授
Gao Minglu: critic, curator, founder of the "Yi Pai" theory. Harvard Ph.D. and currently is a research professor at the Department of History of Art & Architecture at University of Pittsburgh in the USA

迪迪埃·赫希：法国收藏家
Didier Hirsch: French collector

邹跃进：中央美术学院教授，美术史系主任，博士生导师
Zou Yuejin: professor, director of the Art History Department, supervisor of doctoral candidates at the Central Academy of Fine Arts

张文海：批评家
Zhang Wenhai: critic

罗宾·佩卡姆：美国独立批评家，策展人
Robin Peckham: independent critic, curator in the USA

鲍栋：独立批评家，策展人
Bao Dong: independent critic, curator

赵冰：武汉大学教授，博士生导师
Zhao Bing: professor and supervisor of doctoral candidates at Wuhan University

巴巴拉·罗曼：欧洲批评家
Barbara Rollman: critic in Europe

冯·彼得·米夏茨克：欧洲自由批评家，记者
Von Peter Michalzik: independent critic, journalist in Europe

克劳迪亚·泰布勒：德国批评家
Claudia Teibler: critic in Germany

萨比内·阿德勒：德国记者，作家
Sabine Adler: journalist, writer in Germany

高岭：批评家，策展人，《批评家》编辑部主任
Gao Ling: critic, curator, director of the Editorial Department of Art Critic

王璜生：批评家，策展人，中央美术学院美术馆馆长
Wang Huangsheng: critic, curator, director of the Art Museum of China Central Academy of Fine Arts

英格·林德曼：德国艺术经纪人
Inge Lindemann: art dealer in Germany

青宇：自由艺术家
Qing Yu: independent artist

莫里斯·塔普林格：美国纽约《画廊与工作室》批评家
Maurice Taplinger: critic at Gallery & Studio in New York

亚当·唐纳德：美国《纽约艺术杂志》批评家
Adam Donald: critic at NY Arts magazine in New York

杨卫：批评家，策展人，宋庄艺术促进会艺术总监
Yang Wei: critic, curator, art director of Songzhuang Art Promotion Association

威廉·J. 希伊：纽约艺术经纪人
William J. Sheehy: art dealer in New York

王春辰：批评家，策展人，中央美术学院美术馆研究员
Wang Chunchen: critic, curator, researcher at Art Museum of China Central Academy of Fine Arts

吕品田：中国艺术研究院研究员，博士生导师
Lv Pingtian: researcher, supervisor of doctoral candidates at Chinese National Academy of Arts

梅墨生：中国国家画院批评家，书画家
Mei Mosheng: critic, painter and calligrapher at China National Academy of Painting

埃德·麦科马克：美国纽约《画廊与工作室》批评家
Ed McCormack: critic of Gallery & Studio in New York

赵一凡：哈佛大学博士，中国社会科学院外国文学研究所所长，研究员，博士生导师
Zhao Yifan: doctor of Harvard Ph.D. president, researcher and supervisor of doctoral candidates at the Institute of Foreign Literature of the Chinese Academy of Social Sciences

李正天：艺术家，哲学家，广州美术学院油画系教授
Li Zhengtian: artist, philosopher, professor of oil Department at the Guangzhou Academy of Fine Arts

吴鸿：批评家，策展人，"艺术国际"总编
Wu Hong: critic, curator, chief editor of Artintern.net

贾方舟：批评家，策展人，上苑艺术馆常务委员
Jia Fangzhou: critic, curator, permanent member of Art Committee of Shangyuan Art Museum

张晴：批评家，策展人，上海美术馆副馆长
Zhang Qing: critic, curator, vice-director of Shanghai Museum of Art

图书在版编目（CIP）数据

胡志颖作品集/胡志颖著.—福州：海风山版社.
2011.9
ISBN 978-7-5512-0029-5

Ⅰ.①胡… Ⅱ.①胡… Ⅲ.①油画—作品集—中国—
现代Ⅳ.①J223

中国版本图书馆CIP数据核字（2011）第174286号

胡 志 颖 作 品 集
A Collection of Works by Hu Zhiying

作　　者	胡志颖
责任编辑	蓝光耀　朱　军
出版发行	海风出版社
	（福州市鼓东路187号　邮政编码　350001）
出 版 人	焦红辉
印　　刷	深圳雅昌彩色印刷有限公司
开　　本	787×1092mm　1/8
印　　张	31印张
图　　片	160 幅
字　　数	80 千字
印　　数	1—1000册
版　　次	2011年9月第1版
印　　次	2011年9月第1次印刷
书　　号	ISBN 978-7-5512-0029-5/J · 208
定　　价	328.00元